Day Wc

Brecon Beacons

20 circular routes in South Wales

Design and production by Vertebrate Publishing, Sheffield
www.v-publishing.co.uk

Day Walks in the Brecon Beacons

20 circular routes in South Wales

Written by
Harri Roberts

Day Walks in the Brecon Beacons

20 circular routes in South Wales

First published in 2013 by **Vertebrate Publishing.**
Reprinted with minor amendments in 2016.

ISBN 978-1-906148-62-1

Cover photo: Twmpa or Lord Hereford's Knob from Hay Bluff. Photo: Adam Long.
Back cover photo: Cribyn from Pen y Fan. Photo: Adam Long.

Photography by **Adam Long, Adrian Long and Tracy Burton.**

Design by Nathan Ryder, production by Rod Harrison.
www.**v-publishing**.co.uk
Printed and bound in Europe by Pulsio.

FSC www.fsc.org
MIX
Paper from responsible sources
FSC® C128169

Contents

* Shortcut available

BLACK DARREN FROM THE BLACK HILL PHOTO: ADAM LONG

Introduction

Extending for some 70km (45 miles) across the south of Wales, the Brecon Beacons National Park contains an astonishing variety of landscapes. There are spectacular peaks and escarpments, high moorland, peaceful farming valleys, beautiful waterfalls and deep wooded gorges, all within easy reach of major population centres in South Wales and the English Midlands.

The name of the park is misleading, referring historically only to a group of peaks either side of Pen y Fan (886m) – the highest Welsh summit south of Cadair Idris. Connecting the peaks is a spectacular and accessible escarpment path. Justifiably popular, this skyline walk is best avoided on weekends and school holidays.

Fortunately, there are many delightful areas far less frequented. To the west, Fforest Fawr and the Black Mountain are both areas of extensive upland and form the core of the recently designated Fforest Fawr Geopark. Parts of the Black Mountain in particular are extremely remote, though the recent opening of the long-distance Beacons Way has made this area much more accessible. Nevertheless, only Fan Brycheiniog (802m), the highest peak in the range, attracts significant numbers of walkers.

To the north-east, the confusingly named Black Mountains form a distinct geographic region, separated from other upland areas by the broad valley of the River Usk. While the area covered by the mountains is not particularly large, interlocking ridges and deep river valleys create a sense of isolation. The Hatterall ridge, which provides the route for Offa's Dyke Path, marks the National Park boundary and the Wales–England border.

There are also a number of smaller regions with distinct geographic characteristics, the most popular being the 'waterfall country' around Ystradfellte. Among many spectacular waterfalls in this region is Sgwd yr Eira, where walkers can descend the cliffs to pass behind a curtain of cascading water.

Mynydd Llangynidr and Mynydd Llangatwg are two names for one wide expanse of untamed upland, riddled with shake holes and rocky outcrops. Striking limestone cliffs delimit the northeast edge and the entrance to an extensive cave system.

Industrial relics dominate the Blorenge mountain to the south-east. Riddled with old tramroads and former workings, the mountain forms part of the Blaenavon World Heritage Site, described by the designating body UNESCO as 'one of the finest surviving examples in the world of a landscape created by coal mining and iron making'. Contouring around the lower slopes are the tranquil waters of the Monmouthshire & Brecon Canal, possibly the most scenic man-made waterway in Britain.

There are many popular walking routes in the Brecon Beacons that appear time and again in guides to the area. While not ignoring these 'classic' routes, I have tried to strike a balance between justifiably popular walks and those equally deserving but less well known. Even if you have walked the Brecon Beacons before, I hope this book will provide a fresh perspective on the region and lead to places you have yet to discover.

Harri Roberts

Acknowledgements

I would like to thank my partner, Tracy Burton, for casting an experienced editorial eye over the finished manuscript, providing cheer and company on the walks themselves, and for not complaining – too much – when the weather took a turn for the worse.

About the walks

The walks described in this guide are between 7 and 16.5 miles in length and will take around four to eight hours to complete at a leisurely pace. In the case of some of the longer walks, shortcuts providing less demanding routes have been suggested. These are clearly marked on the map and in the route description.

On the whole, the walks follow clear upland paths or waymarked trails through fields and woodland, as well as tracks and quiet country lanes. Where a walk uses an undefined path or route finding is difficult, this is mentioned in the summary for the walk. It is always a good idea to study this carefully, along with the detailed route description, before setting out.

Although the walks vary in terms of length and difficulty, they should all be within the capabilities of a reasonably fit walker. Bear in mind, however, that a number of walks contain lengthy and strenuous ascents. Where appropriate, alternative routes have been described to reduce the amount of overall height gain.

Walk times

The times given are reasonably generous while giving a guideline for planning purposes. If you're unsure how fast or slow you walk, start off with one of the shorter routes and progress to the longer ones once you're sure.

Navigation

As a rule, the description and map included should be enough to get around safely and accurately, but it's always worth carrying a back-up copy of the relevant OS or Harvey Map, in case you inadvertently travel off the page, or need to change your route for any reason.

The Brecon Beacons National Park is covered by the following maps:
Ordnance Survey Explorer OL12 (1:25,000) Brecon Beacons National Park Western Area
Ordnance Survey Explorer OL13 (1:25,000) Brecon Beacons National Park Eastern Area

Harvey/BMC British Mountain Map Brecon Beacons (1:40,000)

A compass and the basic ability to use it should be seen as prerequisite to walking in the mountains even if you are carrying a GPS.

GPS

A GPS can be a useful navigational aid and is well worth carrying. But always carry spare batteries – they do tend to run out at the worst times – and always carry a map and compass as back up.

Mobile phones

Mobile phone reception is at best iffy in the mountains so it's definitely best not to rely on it. If you do need to make contact with emergency services, try heading up towards a summit, where you often have more chance of a signal.

Footpaths and rights of way

The walks in this book all follow rights of way, permissive paths or cross open access land.

Comfort

A decent pair of boots will protect your feet from the kind of terrain experienced in mountains and will also provide ankle support, waterproofing and grip on steep slopes. And a waterproof jacket could be useful on any day at any time of year. A pack containing a waterproof, spare layer and some food and drink, will make any day more comfortable. Anybody with joint problems, for example ankles or knees, will probably benefit from a pair of trekking poles.

Safety

Mountain weather changes quickly and unexpectedly, if you are in any doubt, it's probably best not to start, and if you do get caught out, it's always better to back off your route rather than carry on regardless. The mountains will always be there. In winter, consider carrying a torch in case the light fades before you get off the hill – it's difficult reading a map in the dark.

Mountain Rescue

In case of an emergency dial **999** and ask for **Police** and then **Mountain Rescue**. Where possible give a six-figure grid reference of your location or that of the casualty. If you don't have reception where you are, try and attract the help of others around you. The usual distress signal is six short blasts on a whistle every minute. If you don't have a whistle, then shouting may work.

Mountain Rescue by SMS text

Another option in the UK is contacting the emergency services by SMS text – useful if you have a low battery or intermittent signal, but you do need to register your phone first. To register, simply text **'register'** to 999 and then follow the instructions in the reply. Do it now – it could save yours or someone else's life. **www.emergencysms.org.uk**

THE SOUTH RIDGE OF YSGYRYD FAWR PHOTO: ADAM LONG

The Countryside Code

Be safe – plan ahead

Even when going out locally, it's best to get the latest information about where and when you can go; for example, your rights to go onto some areas of open land may be restricted while work is carried out, for safety reasons or during breeding and shooting seasons. Follow advice and local signs, and be prepared for the unexpected.

» Refer to up-to-date maps or guidebooks.

» You're responsible for your own safety and for others in your care, so be prepared for changes in weather and other events.

» There are many organisations offering specific advice on equipment and safety, or contact visitor information centres and libraries for a list of outdoor recreation groups.

» Check weather forecasts before you leave, and don't be afraid to turn back.

» Part of the appeal of the countryside is that you can get away from it all. You may not see anyone for hours and there are many places without clear mobile phone signals, so let someone else know where you're going and when you expect to return.

Leave gates and property as you find them

Please respect the working life of the countryside, as our actions can affect people's livelihoods, our heritage, and the safety and welfare of animals and ourselves.

» A farmer will normally leave a gate closed to keep livestock in, but may sometimes leave it open so they can reach food and water. Leave gates as you find them or follow instructions on signs; if walking in a group, make sure the last person knows how to leave the gates.

» In fields where crops are growing, follow the paths wherever possible.

» Use gates and stiles wherever possible – climbing over walls, hedges and fences can damage them and increase the risk of farm animals escaping.

» Our heritage belongs to all of us – be careful not to disturb ruins and historic sites.

» Leave machinery and livestock alone – don't interfere with animals even if you think they're in distress. Try to alert the farmer instead.

Protect plants and animals, and take your litter home

We have a responsibility to protect our countryside now and for future generations, so make sure you don't harm animals, birds, plants or trees.

- Litter and leftover food doesn't just spoil the beauty of the countryside, it can be dangerous to wildlife and farm animals and can spread disease – so take your litter home with you. Dropping litter and dumping rubbish are criminal offences.
- Discover the beauty of the natural environment and take special care not to damage, destroy or remove features such as rocks, plants and trees. They provide homes and food for wildlife, and add to everybody's enjoyment of the countryside.
- Wild animals and farm animals can behave unpredictably if you get too close, especially if they're with their young – so give them plenty of space.
- Fires can be as devastating to wildlife and habitats as they are to people and property – so be careful not to drop a match or smouldering cigarette at any time of the year. Sometimes, controlled fires are used to manage vegetation, particularly on heaths and moors between October and early April, so please check that a fire is not supervised before calling 999.

Keep dogs under close control

The countryside is a great place to exercise dogs, but it is the owner's duty to make sure their dog is not a danger or nuisance to farm animals, wildlife or other people.

- By law, you must control your dog so that it does not disturb or scare farm animals or wildlife. You must keep your dog on a short lead on most areas of open country and common land between 1 March and 31 July, and at all times near farm animals.
- You do not have to put your dog on a lead on public paths as long as it is under close control. But as a general rule, keep your dog on a lead if you cannot rely on its obedience. By law, farmers are entitled to destroy a dog that injures or worries their animals.
- If a farm animal chases you and your dog, it is safer to let your dog off the lead – don't risk getting hurt by trying to protect it.
- Take particular care that your dog doesn't scare sheep and lambs or wander where it might disturb birds that nest on the ground and other wildlife – eggs and young will soon die without protection from their parents.
- Everyone knows how unpleasant dog mess is and it can cause infections – so always clean up after your dog and get rid of the mess responsibly. Also make sure your dog is wormed regularly.

Consider other people

Showing consideration and respect for other people makes the countryside a pleasant environment for everyone – at home, at work and at leisure.

- Busy traffic on small country roads can be unpleasant and dangerous to local people, visitors and wildlife – so slow down and, where possible, leave your vehicle at home, consider sharing lifts and use alternatives such as public transport or cycling. For public transport information, phone Traveline on 0871 200 2233.
- Respect the needs of local people – for example, don't block gateways, driveways or other entry points with your vehicle.
- By law, cyclists must give way to walkers and horse riders on bridleways.
- Keep out of the way when farm animals are being gathered or moved and follow directions from the farmer.
- Support the rural economy – for example, buy your supplies from local shops.

How to use this book

This book should provide you with all of the information that you need for an enjoyable, trouble free and successful walk. The following tips should also be of help:

1. We strongly recommend that you invest in the maps listed above on page ix. These are essential even if you are familiar with the area – you may need to cut short the walk or take an alternative route.

2. Choose your route. Consider the time you have available and the abilities/level of experience of all of members your party – then read the safety section of this guide.

3. We recommend that you study the route description carefully before setting off. Cross-reference this with your map so that you've got a good sense of general orientation in case you need an escape route. Make sure that you are familiar with the symbols used on the maps.

4. Get out there and get walking!

Maps, descriptions, distances

While every effort has been made to maintain accuracy within the maps and descriptions in this guide, we have had to process a vast amount of information and we are unable to guarantee that every single detail is correct.

Please exercise caution if a direction appears at odds with the route on the map. If in doubt, a comparison between the route, the description and a quick cross-reference with your map (along with a bit of common sense) should help ensure that you're on the right track. Note that distances have been measured off the map, and map distances rarely coincide 100% with distances on the ground. Please treat stated distances as a guideline only.

Ordnance Survey maps are the most commonly used, are easy to read and many people are happy using them. If you're not familiar with OS maps and are unsure of what the symbols mean, you can download a free OS 1:25,000 map legend from **www.v-outdoor.co.uk**

Here are a few of the symbols and abbreviations we use on the maps and in our directions:

S ROUTE STARTING POINT

2 ROUTE MARKER

OR OPTIONAL ROUTE

SC SHORT CUT

52 ADDITIONAL GRID LINE NUMBERS TO AID NAVIGATION

PB = public bridleway; **PF** = public footpath; **GR** = grid reference.

Km/mile conversion chart

Metric to Imperial

1 kilometre [km]	1000 m	0.6214 mile
1 metre [m]	100 cm	1.0936 yd
1 centimetre [cm]	10 mm	0.3937 in
1 millimetre [mm]		0.03937 in

Imperial to Metric

1 mile	1760 yd	1.6093 km
1 yard [yd]	3 ft	0.9144 m
1 foot [ft]	12 in	0.3048 m
1 inch [in]		2.54 cm

The main peaks of the Brecon Beacons: Pen y Fan and Corn Du.
photo © Drew Buckley

Welsh place names

Welsh place names are often descriptive, so knowing what names mean can be a great help when walking. Unfortunately, providing a glossary of Welsh place name elements is complicated by a grammatical feature of Welsh known as mutation, in which the initial consonants of words vary. The following list includes mutated and unmutated forms of some of the more common place name elements you are likely to come across.

RED KITE PHOTO: ADAM LONG

aber	estuary, confluence
afon	river
bach/fach	small
betws	house of prayer
blaen	head of a valley
bryn	hill
bwlch	pass or gap
cae	field
caer/gaer	fort, fortified camp
capel	chapel
carn/garn	cairn or pile of stones
carreg/garreg	stone
castell	castle
cefn	ridge
coch/goch	red
coed	wood
craig/graig	crag
cwm	valley
dŵr	water
dyffryn	valley
eglwys	church
esgair	ridge
ffordd	road
ffridd	pasture
ffynnon	well or spring
glan/lan	bank or shore
glyn	deep valley
gwaun/waun	moorland or meadow
hafod	summer farmstead
hen	old
isaf	lower
llan	church, sacred enclosure
llwyn	bush or grove
llyn	lake
maen	stone
maes	field
mawr/fawr	big
moel/foel	bare hill
mynydd	mountain
nant	stream
pant	hollow
pen	top or end
pentre	village
plas	hall, mansion
pont/bont	bridge
pwll	pool
rhiw	slope
rhos	moorland
rhyd	ford
tal	end or front
tan/dan	below
tarren/darren	escarpment
tref/dref	homestead or town
tŷ	house
y/yr	the
ynys	island
ystrad	wide valley

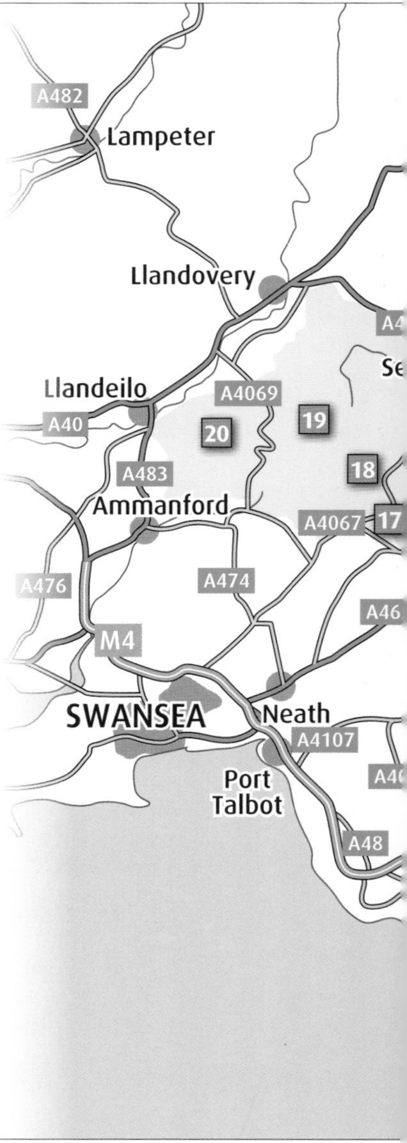

A482
Lampeter
Llandovery
Llandeilo
A4069
A40
20
19
18
A483
Ammanford
A4067
17
A476
A474
M4
SWANSEA
Neath
A4107
Port Talbot
A48

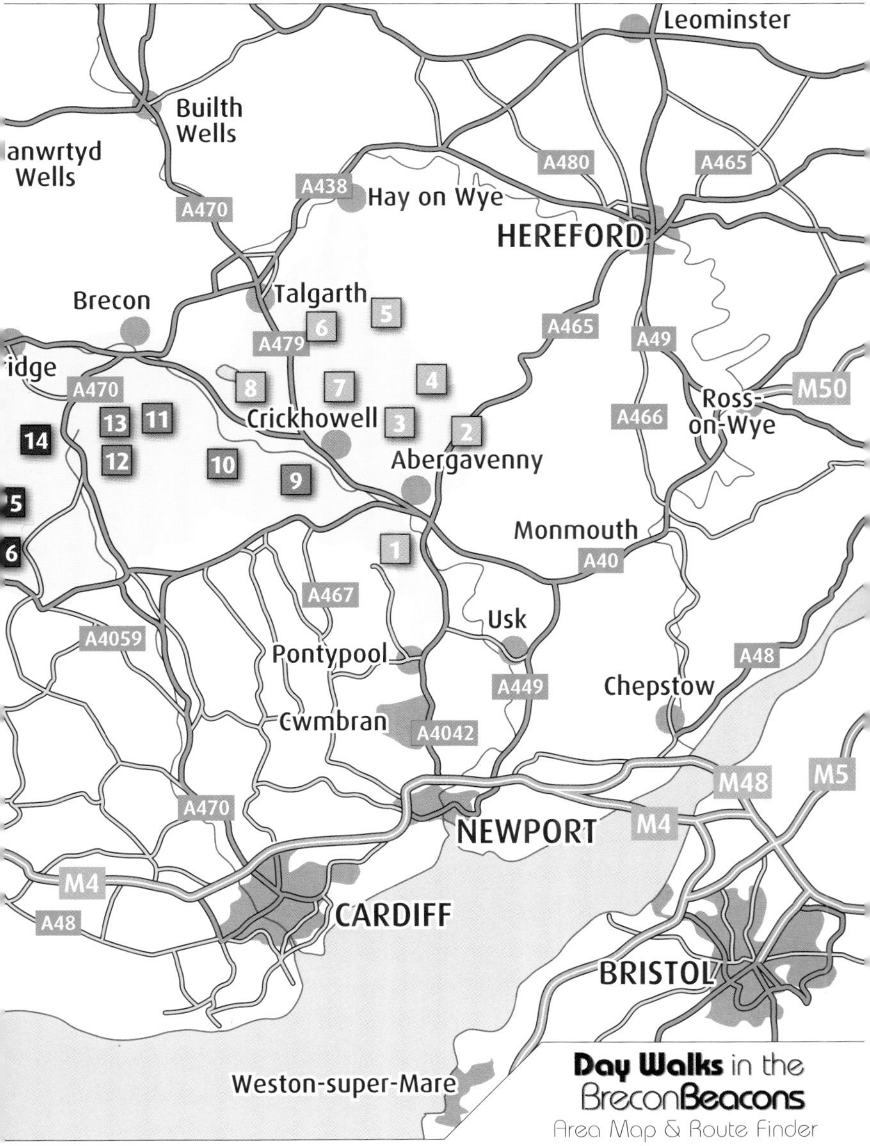
Leominster
Builth Wells
anwrtyd Wells
A470
A438
Hay on Wye
A480
A465
HEREFORD
Brecon
Talgarth
5
6
A479
A465
A49
idge
A470
8
7
4
M50
13
11
Crickhowell
3
2
A466
Ross-on-Wye
14
12
10
9
Abergavenny
5
Monmouth
6
1
A40
A467
Usk
A4059
Pontypool
A48
A449
Chepstow
Cwmbran
A4042
M48
M5
A470
NEWPORT
M4
M4
CARDIFF
A48
BRISTOL
Weston-super-Mare
Day Walks in the Brecon Beacons
Area Map & Route Finder

SECTION 1

Blorenge & the Black Mountains

The Black Mountains form a distinct geographic region separated from other upland areas by the broad valley of the Usk. The Black Mountains 'hand' – five parallel ridges extending from an escarpment 'wrist' – creates a particularly good landscape for devising circular walks. Beautiful river valleys run between each 'finger', while just outside the 'hand' lie a number of outlying peaks and the largest natural lake in South Wales – Llangors Lake. Also included in this section is the Blorenge, a fine mountain separated from the rest of the National Park by the deep cleft of Clydach Gorge. The mountain straddles the border between rural and industrial Wales and contains a former industrial landscape of international significance.

THE LLANBEDR HORSESHOE FROM THE AIR *PHOTO: ADRIAN LONG*

SUNRISE BEHIND CRICKHOWELL AND THE SUGAR LOAF. PHOTO: ADAM LONG

YSGYRYD FAWR FROM ABOVE THE PUNCHBOWL, BLORENGE PHOTO: ADAM LONG

01 A Circuit of the Blorenge

11.5km/7.1miles

Well-marked paths around Wales' 'Iron Mountain'.

Pen-ffordd-goch Pond » Cwm Ifor » Garn Ddyrys » Cwm Craf » Punchbowl » Blorenge (561m) » Pen-ffordd-goch Pond

Start

Keeper's Pond car park at the southern end of Pen-ffordd-goch Pond. This is on the B4246 just north of Blaenavon. GR: SO 254107.

The Walk

The Brecon Beacons National Park is not just an area of great natural beauty; its south-eastern corner around the Blorenge mountain also contains one of the most significant early industrial landscapes in the world. There is everything here: the mountain is riddled with old tramroads, tunnels, forges, scouring ponds and channels, making it a unique and fascinating environment in which to walk. Indeed, the area around Blaenavon is one of only nine in the world identified by UNESCO as offering 'a complete example of an industrial landscape', a critical factor in its designation as a World Heritage Site.

Our walk begins in the Keeper's Pond car park, marked on OS maps by its original Welsh name, Pen-ffordd-goch ('head of the red road'). After following a path around the lake, we head steeply downhill on an old road known as Rhiw Ifor to meet up with Hill's Tramroad. This level grassy path snakes around the slopes of Cwm Llanwenarth to Garn Ddyrys, where the foundations of a major foundry can be traced.

An easy, level path continues along the northern slopes of the Blorenge to Cwm Craf. Here the former tramroad turns steeply downhill towards Llanfoist Wharf, but we continue around the base of the common to the Punchbowl. This spectacular bowl-shaped valley and pond was once the venue for illegal bare-knuckle fights, but now makes a fine sheltered picnic spot.

After a steep climb along a beech-lined track, we double back across open mountainside to the top of the Cwm Craf escarpment – a steeply plunging slope offering the most spectacular views of the day. A path leads past the summit to the Foxhunter car park, named after a famous Olympic showjumper. Easy paths to the south of the road take us back to our starting point.

A CIRCUIT OF THE BLORENGE

DISTANCE: 11.5KM/7.1MILES » **TOTAL ASCENT:** 466M/1,529FT » **START GR:** SO 254107 » **TIME:** ALLOW 4 HOURS **MAP:** OS EXPLORER OL13 BRECON BEACONS NATIONAL PARK EASTERN AREA » **REFRESHMENTS:** NONE ON ROUTE; NEAREST PUB IS THE LAMB AND FOX, PWLL-DU » **NAVIGATION:** EASY AND WELL MARKED

PEN-FFORDD-GOCH POND PHOTO: ADAM LONG

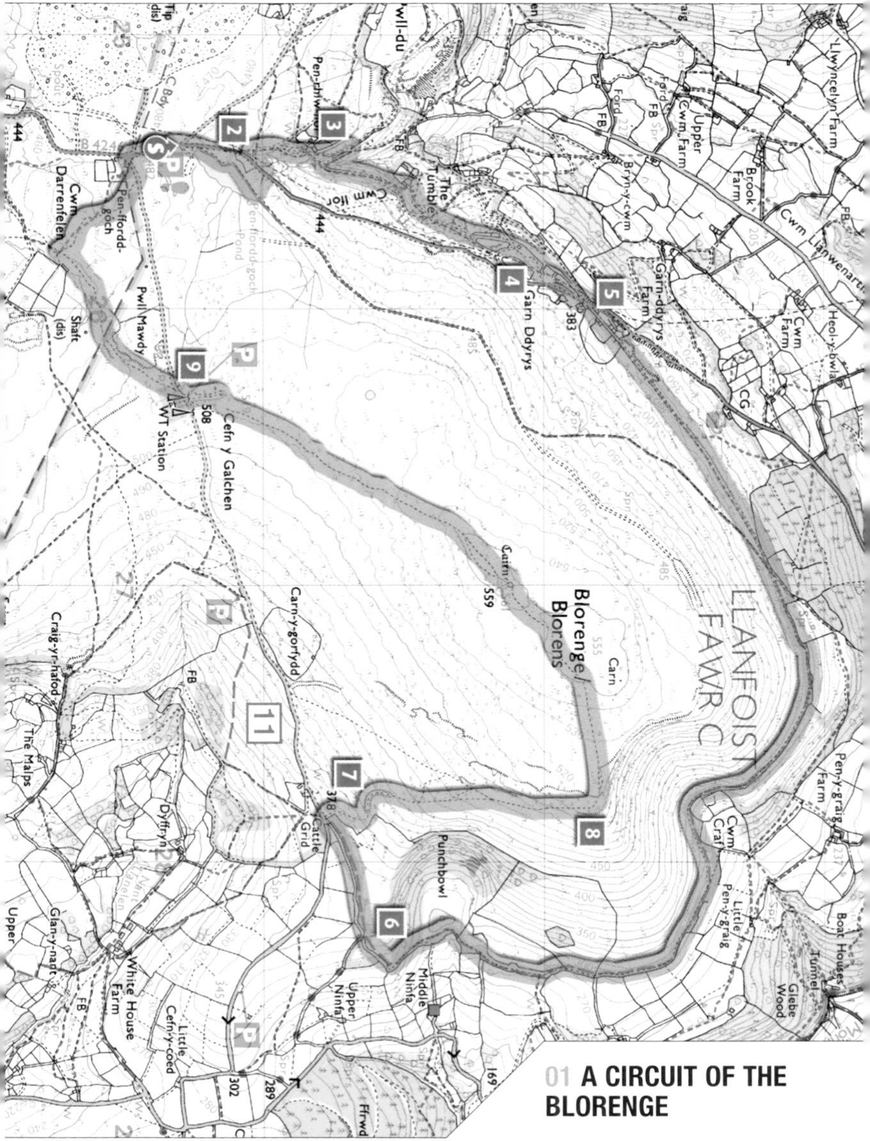

01 A CIRCUIT OF THE BLORENGE

Directions – A Circuit of the Blorenge

S From the car park, follow the path around the edge of the lake. Just before a wooden footbridge at the end of the lake, **turn left** on a rough path and descend to the main road. **Bear left** across the road to a wooden signpost.

2 Follow the arrow in the direction of *Garn Ddyrys*, shortly **curving right** to reach a signed fork. Take the **right-hand path**, signed *Cwm Llanwenarth*, and descend steeply.

3 At a junction with a level grassy path crossroads (Hill's Tramroad), **turn right**, signed *Garn Ddyrys*. Cross a footbridge over a stream and continue across the slopes of Cwm Llanwenarth. Pass a misshapen pile of slag and follow the tramroad through the overgrown foundations of the former Garn Ddyrys foundry.

4 **Ignore** the track bearing right and follow a waymark arrow **straight ahead** between electricity wires and a fence. **Bear right** slightly, to pass below the wires, and follow a grassy path up to a road. Cross over and continue across open ground with the road below. Pass to the left of a stone enclosure and drop to a waymark post with *Llanfoist* signed to **the right**.

5 You are now back on Hill's Tramroad, following a level, easy path across the lower slopes of the Blorenge. After passing round the head of Cwm Craf, the path leaves the tramroad (which heads steeply downhill to Llanfoist) and descends diagonally across the hill. **Ignore** a stile below and keep **straight ahead** on the main path to join a grassy track along the base of the common. Eventually pass through a gate marking the boundary of a Woodland Trust reserve and descend to a small lake called the Punchbowl.

6 Climb steeply from the Punchbowl on a track lined with beeches. Before leaving the trees, the track curves right, climbing steadily across more open ground to reach a tarmac lane.

7 **Ignore** the road and turn **sharp right** onto the mountain, signed *Blorenge*. Initially, the path stays close to a drystone wall, but climbs steeply away at a corner. After about 200m, **bear right** along a sunken gully, which continues upwards to a wider grassy track. Follow the escarpment edge above Cwm Craf, enjoying fantastic views across the Usk Valley.

8 At a stone hut, **bear left**, away from the escarpment, and follow a rough track heading gently uphill to the summit. Keep **straight ahead** past the trig point marker and join an obvious path, now surfaced in places, in the direction of two masts.

9 Keep **straight ahead** through the Foxhunter car park. Cross the road and join a path to the right of the two masts. Follow the path gently downhill to a waymark post. **Turn right** onto the path signed *Keeper's Pond*. Go through a narrow gully and follow the waymarked path as it curves right. Your path is now roughly parallel to the B4246 away on the left. On reaching a lane, **turn left** towards a junction with the B4246. **Turn right** and follow the grass verge back to the car park.

BLORENGE SUMMIT PHOTO: ADAM LONG

THE LANDSLIP ON THE WEST SIDE OF YSGYRYD FAWR PHOTO: ADAM LONG

02 Ysgyryd Fawr & Bryn Arw

17.4km/10.8miles

Abergavenny's 'Holy Mountain' and a little-walked hill on the edge of the Black Mountains.

B4521 » Ysgyryd Fawr (486m) » Llanvihangel Crucorney » Stanton » Bryn Arw (384m) » B4521

Start

Lay-by on the B4521 south of Ysgyryd Fawr. GR: SO 328164.

The Walk

Though by no means the loftiest of the Black Mountains peaks, these two outlying summits still form an impressive gateway to the Gafenni valley. Their slender ridges also offer some of the most spectacular skyline walking in the National Park.

Our walk begins from a lay-by at the southern end of Ysgyryd Fawr, the higher of the two summits and a mountain steeped in legend and folklore. (Locally, the mountain is generally referred to in anglicised form as 'The Skirrid'.) The mountain's distinctive shape – the result of landslips during the last Ice Age – is popularly attributed to either an earthquake at the time of Jesus's crucifixion or the keel of Noah's ark scraping across the mountain top. Secret Catholic services were once held in a small stone chapel on the summit.

After a steep climb, a breathtaking ridge walk leads to the north end of the mountain and a trig point marking the summit. To avoid a steep descent, we retrace our steps to a more gentle route down and begin a long descent to Llanvihangel Crucorney. This pleasant village gives us an opportunity to visit the Skirrid Inn, a pub which claims to be not only the oldest in Wales but also the most haunted.

An attractive woodland path leads to Stanton, where we cross into the narrow side valley of Cwm Coedycerrig and begin to ascend the northern slopes of Bryn Arw. Another delightful skyline walk takes us to the southern end of the mountain and a descent into a secluded wooded valley.

The valley soon opens out and we head back across fields towards the distinctive shape of Ysgyryd Fawr. A field path skirting the mountain offers a pleasant and easy return to our starting point.

YSGYRYD FAWR & BRYN ARW

DISTANCE: 17.4KM/10.8MILES » **TOTAL ASCENT:** 688M/2,257FT » **START GR:** SO 328164 » **TIME:** ALLOW 6 HOURS
MAP: OS EXPLORER OL13, BRECON BEACONS NATIONAL PARK EASTERN AREA, 1:25,000 » **REFRESHMENTS:** SKIRRID MOUNTAIN INN, LLANVIHANGEL CRUCORNEY » **NAVIGATION:** GENERALLY WELL SIGNED BUT SOME MAP WORK MAY BE REQUIRED.

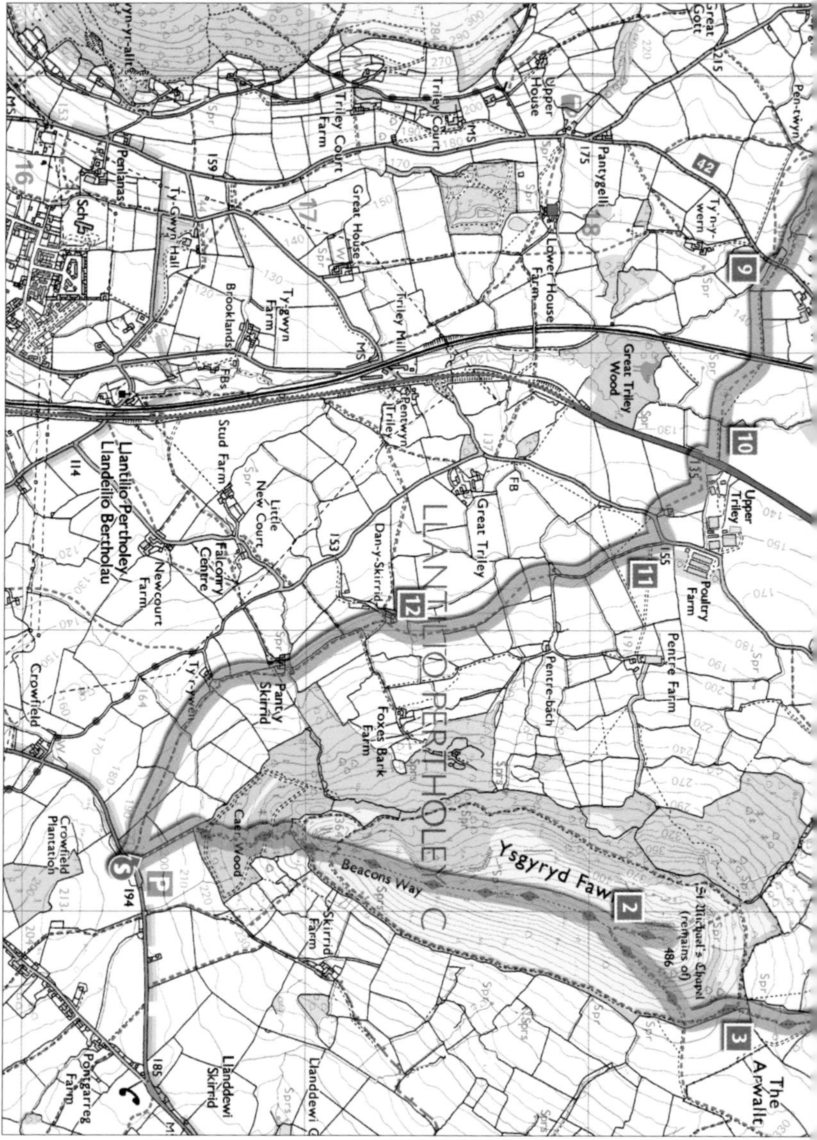

Llantilio Pertholey/
Llandeilio Bertholau
LLANTILIO PERTHOLEY C
Ysgyryd Fawr
Beacons Way
St Michael's Chapel
(remains of)
486
The
Arwallt
Great Triley
Great Triley
Wood
Upper
Triley
Poultry
Farm
Pentre Farm
Pentre-bach
Foxes Bank
Farm
Dan-y-Skirrid
Pant-y-
Skirrid
Ty'r-ywen
Crowfield
Crowfield
Plantation
Caer Wood
Skirrid
Farm
Llanddewi
Skirrid
Pontgarreg
Farm
Newcourt
Farm
Falconry
Centre
Little
New Court
Stud Farm
Pentwyn
Trilley
Triley Mill
Brooklands
Ty-gwyn
Farm
Great House
Ty-Gwyn Hall
Penlanas
Sch
Triley Court
Farm
Triley Court
Upper
House
Pantygelli
Lower House
Farm
Ty'n-y-
wern
Pen-twyn
Great
Gott
16
17
18
42
2
3
9
10
11
12
S
P

02 YSGYRYD FAWR & BRYN ARW

Directions – Ysgyryd Fawr & Bryn Arw

S Pass through a metal barrier and follow a gravel track up the hill. Enter Caer Wood and **fork right**. Climb steeply, crossing two grassy forest tracks, and reach a gate in a mossy dry-stone wall. Go through the gate and **turn right**, alongside the wall. **Fork left** uphill and climb steeply, then **swing right** to an area of open ground. **Bear left** and follow the ridge north to the summit trig point.

2 **Return** along the ridge for about 200m and **turn sharp left**, onto a clear grassy path descending diagonally across the hill. At a point parallel with the northern end of the mountain, **turn right** onto a waymarked path down to the bottom edge of the common. **Turn left** along the fence to a gate.

3 Still descending, follow *Beacons Way* markers through fields to a lane. **Turn right** along the road for about 500m, then **left** onto a footpath signed *Crucorney*. Cross fields and enter a small wood. Leave the wood by a footbridge and cross a further field. Follow a fence towards a ramshackle barn.

4 Meet a track to the right of the barn and **turn left**. Pass Llanvihangel Court and follow the access road down to the A465. Cross carefully and continue up a short section of concrete track to a church. **Turn right** along a road, passing the *Skirrid Inn*. Just past the pub, **turn left** down a road signed *Cwmyoy* and *Llanthony*. At the bottom of the hill, **bear right** (Longtown) and cross a river. **Turn left** at the first footpath, signed *Hatterrall Hill*.

5 Follow the field edge to a railway line and cross carefully. **Bear right** in the next field, then climb **steeply left**. Cross a stile into a farmyard and **turn left**. Leaving the Beacons Way, **fork left** between barns and head across a field to an area of newly planted trees. Where directed, **turn right** onto a smaller path and keep **straight ahead** to Strawberry Cottage Wood. Descend steadily along the woodland edge to a field in front of Strawberry Cottage.

6 Cross the field to a footbridge over Afon Honddu. **Bear left** across a road and up a dead-end lane. Continue past a farm on a surfaced track and climb gently to a gate, marked *Bryn Arw*. A bit further on, **fork right** and climb past a sign for *Bettws* and *Pantigelli*. The track swings left, to a gate onto Bryn Arw Common.

7 **Turn left** and handrail the common boundary up the hill. At a path crossroads near a wooden stile, **turn right** onto a level path. **Bear left**, climbing diagonally. The path is vague in places, but eventually swings left to meet a more defined path on the ridge. **Turn left** and follow the crest of the ridge as it curves right.

8 Where the ridge ends, **bear left** past an isolated tree, then **swing right** along a grassy ledge below the ridge's 'snout'. **Fork left**, towards the common fence, then **bear left** to follow the fence steeply downhill into a narrow valley. At the bottom, **turn left** onto a gravel track and go past a cottage onto a woodland path above a stream. **Ignore** a ford and keep **straight ahead** across a bank to a stile. Continue along a grassy track by the stream to a road by a house.

9 **Turn right** at the road, then **immediately left** through an unmarked field gate opposite the house. Cross to another gate, then follow the left edge of a field to a stile in the corner (Ysgyryd Fawr should be directly ahead). Cross the railway line and **bear slightly right** across a large field to a stile. Follow a grassy track up to the A465 and **turn right** along the grass verge.

10 Cross to a stile and keep **straight ahead** up a field until level with the last building on the left. **Turn right** and cross the field to a stile in front of a house. Follow a track up to a lane and **turn left**.

11 At a left-hand bend, **turn right** onto a dead-end lane signed *Llanddewi Skirrid*. Where the track ends at Top Cottage, **continue ahead** onto a waymarked field path below Ysgyryd Fawr. Follow the direction of each waymark arrow carefully.

12 Cross a track near the next house and **turn left** as directed. **Ignore** a stile on the right and keep **straight ahead** along the bottom edge of the field to a stile at the far end. Pass two more houses, then start **bearing left**. Follow waymarks carefully back to the car park at the southern end of the mountain.

SUGAR LOAF FROM YSGYRYD FAWR PHOTO: ADAM LONG

03 The Sugar Loaf & Crug Mawr 19.8km/12.3miles

Two splendid tops and a hidden treasure in the heart of the Black Mountains.

Bettws/Forest Coal Pit » Sugar Loaf (596m) » Llanbedr » Crug Mawr (550m) » Partrishow » Coed y Cerrig » Bettws/Forest Coal Pit

Start

Small parking area on the minor road between Bettws and Forest Coal Pit. GR: SO 292200.

The Walk

The Sugar Loaf is a popular mountain most commonly tackled from the south. Approaching from the north-east, we avoid the crowds and are able to incorporate another fine peak, Crug Mawr, into our walk. Between these two upland sections, we cross peaceful river valleys, pass an astonishingly well-preserved medieval church, and follow boardwalks through a diverse and ancient wood. While at times demanding, this is a walk that demonstrates more than any other the tranquillity and varied beauty of the Black Mountains.

We begin from a small parking area off the minor road between Bettws and Forest Coal Pit. A lovely path climbs steadily to the rocky summit of the Sugar Loaf, where there are fantastic views across a wide area of the National Park and Usk Valley. Descending westwards, we drop to the Grwyne Fawr and Grwyne Fechan, two sparkling streams whose wooded banks provide delightful walking. A visit to the Red Lion in the pretty village of Llanbedr is also a possibility.

The second big climb crosses Crug Mawr to St Ishow's Church in Partrishow. Tucked away in its remote mountain valley, this medieval church survived the ravages of the Reformation and contains an amazing medieval rood screen and a chilling 'doom' figure of a skeleton with spade, hourglass and scythe.

Though the big climbs are over, we still have to cross the shoulder of hill between Partrishow and Coed y Cerrig, a National Nature Reserve of diverse woodland. Boardwalks provide a dry and easy route across the marshy valley bottom. A final climb from Coed y Cerrig takes us past the outskirts of Forest Coal Pit and back to our starting point.

THE SUGAR LOAF & CRUG MAWR

DISTANCE: 19.8KM/12.3MILES » **TOTAL ASCENT:** 914M/2,998FT » **START GR:** SO 292200 » **TIME:** ALLOW 6.5 HOURS **MAP:** OS EXPLORER OL13, BRECON BEACONS NATIONAL PARK EASTERN AREA, 1:25,000 » **REFRESHMENTS:** THE RED LION, LLANBEDR; NEAREST OTHER PUB IS THE CROWN, PANTYGELLI » **NAVIGATION:** EASY TO FOLLOW IN FINE WEATHER.

Pentre
Gelli Boeth
Ford
Neuadd-fawr
Glan-yr-afon
Grwyne Fechan
Bont
258
Crug Mawr
550
6
Blaen-Nant Ma
Sunny Bank
234
221
Milaid-uchaf
Cwm Milaid
Beacons Way
Sheepfold
Milaid-isaf
242
Pen-cae
Green Cottage
FB
Llwynon
Graig-lwyd
Blaen-yr-henbant
498
236
Tre-domen
Wern-fâch
FB
Ford
Draen
Gelli-fanw
Cwm Beusych
Graig-fa
5
Ford
Beusych
Draen-fâch
Henbant Fach
Hen-bant-fawr
Ford
Pen-y-beili
Ffynnon-wen
Fords
Fords
26
Fords
168
Glyn-Pedr
Llanbedr
Pen-yr-heol
Upper Cwm Bridge
Gudder
Ford
Dyffryn-ganol
174
4
Pant-teg
148
Dyffryn
183
159
25
Coed Mill
Sewage Works
Pen-y-bont
137
Lower Cwm Bridge
Ford
Pen-lan
Moor Park
185
Cwm-bwch
Gellyrhydd
Ty-Llangenny
Coed Ynys-faen
Ty-cadol
Cwm Bwch
Grwyne Fawr
Gob-pwllau
Mynydd Pen-y-fâl
205
3
Pengilfach
Ty-draw
Standing Stones
186
Cwm
FB

03 THE SUGAR LOAF & CRUG MAWR

Directions – The Sugar Loaf & Crug Mawr

S From the car park, take an enclosed path onto the common signed *Sugar Loaf.* **Bear left** along the common edge and begin to climb. Follow the boundary wall as it curves right and climb to a path junction by a wall corner. **Turn left** for about 200m, still following the wall. Just before the path dips, **fork right** and ascend to a spur. Follow the obvious path towards the Sugar Loaf. At a path crossroads below the summit, keep **straight ahead** to clamber up the last few metres to the top.

2 Pass the trig point and cross a jumble of rock. Once off the top, follow a wide grassy path along the mountain's west spur. **Fork right three times** (the last two times in quick succession) and descend steeply to a wide grassy path contouring around the base of the hill. Cross the path and follow a fence down to a rusty metal gate. A grassy bridleway descends from here to a rough vehicle track. **Turn left** and descend gently to a farm.

3 Follow a lane downhill to the next footpath **on the right**. Waymarks lead across fields to a track in front of Gellyrhydd Farm. **Turn left**, then **right** at the next track, signed *Pen-y-bont.* Take the next footpath **on the left** and descend to a footbridge across the Grwyne Fawr river. Cross a field towards a gate, keeping the smaller Grwyne Fechan river to your left. Cross a lane and another field, and climb onto a shoulder of land above the river. A rough track drops back down to the river. Continue upstream as far as the second bridge on the left.

4 **Turn right** onto a zigzagging path up the side of the wooded valley (or left over the bridge if you wish to detour to Llanbedr). Where the path divides, **fork left** and climb steeply. Continue along a field edge and cross a lane. After a second field, **aim left** of a house and join a track. At a waymark, **turn left** up a steep slope and climb to a junction with a bridleway.

5 **Turn left** and follow a sunken track through woodland to a gate onto the mountain. Follow the common boundary uphill until a sharp right turn. Keep **straight ahead** for a short distance, then **bear right**. The path briefly rejoins the common edge, then **bears left** below the higher ground of Blaen-yr-henbant. Continue along the main path above Cwm Milaid as far as a *Beacons Way* marker at the head of the valley. **Turn right**, in the direction of the arrow, and climb a short, steep slope to the summit of Crug Mawr.

6 Keep **straight ahead** in the direction of a *Beacons Way* arrow. After a pond, the path descends more steeply. **Bear left** near the bottom of the common, keeping a fence to your right. **Fork right** to continue along the fence and descend to a dry-stone wall. **Turn right** and pass through two gates onto a rough enclosed track. Keep **straight ahead** onto a lane and soon after begin to descend steeply.

7 At a sign for *St Ishow's Church*, **turn left** through a metal gate and descend between gravestones. **Turn left** past the church (which is kept open for visitors) and continue through a kissing gate into a field. Keep **straight ahead** to a wall corner above a farmhouse and **turn sharp right**, following the wall downhill to a metal gate. **Turn left** between farm buildings. At the end of the house, **bear left** through a rusty farm gate into a field.

8 Follow *Beacons Way* markers down through fields and past a stone ruin. **Bear left** onto a rough track and drop to a lane. Take the narrow lane opposite signed *Tabernacle Chapel* and cross the Grwyne Fawr river. Leave the Beacons Way by **turning right** onto a lane.

9 Continue past a house onto a grassy track. Climb steadily along the side of the valley to reach another house. Pass behind the house and **keep straight ahead** along the access track. At a lane, **keep straight ahead** across a stone stile opposite and follow the right edge of a field to another stone stile. Cross a track below a small quarry onto a rough track opposite.

10 Cross a road in front of a grand house and join a track below the buildings. Follow a grassy track down to a lake and drop to a stile into woods. Descend through trees, **bearing right** along the main path to a small parking area. Cross a road and join a boardwalk above the marshy valley bottom. Take either fork where the path splits, both branches rejoining. At a rough track, **turn right** and climb back across the wooded slope.

11 At a T-junction with a wider track, **turn right** and follow the track downhill to a lane. **Turn left** at the next vehicle track, signed *Bettws*. Keep ahead at a house onto a short section of grassy track into a field. Follow the left-hand edge, then **aim right**, down to a metal gate in the bottom corner. Join a rough, boggy track along the valley bottom, climbing higher up the bank if this is waterlogged. **Keep straight ahead** at a lane and climb to a T-junction. **Turn right** for about 150m to return to the car park.

LLANTHONY PRIORY, VALE OF EWYAS PHOTO: ADAM LONG

04 Llanthony, Cwmyoy & Hatterrall Hill

13.8km/8.5miles

A ruined abbey and crooked church tower in the beautiful Vale of Ewyas.

Llanthony » Cwmyoy » Hatterrall Hill (531m) » Llanthony

Start

**Free car park at Llanthony Priory.
GR: SO 289278.**

The Walk

Nestling in the beautiful Vale of Ewyas, the splendid ruins of Llanthony Priory provide a fabulous walking base. Founded by a Norman nobleman, William de Lacy, at the beginning of the twelfth century, the priory became one of Wales's great medieval buildings, but fell into decay following the Dissolution of the Monasteries. After centuries of neglect, work has now been carried out to stabilise and protect what remains.

We begin by heading south, an ancient hollow lane taking us past a series of ruined farms (the valley was more heavily populated in the past). After passing below the craggy slopes of the Darren, we descend to St Martin's Church in Cwmyoy – 'the most crooked church in Great Britain'. Local folklore attributes the subsidence which has twisted the church building in all directions to an earthquake at the time of Christ's crucifixion, but the real cause dates back to the time of the last Ice Age, when retreating glaciers caused a large section of the valley wall behind Cwmyoy to collapse. The church was built on the unstable spoil, which continued to shift over the centuries that followed, buckling the walls of the building as it did so.

Heading up Cwm Iau ('valley of the yoke'), we pick up a fine turf path on to Hatterrall Hill. This becomes fainter as we ascend, eventually disappearing altogether; Offa's Dyke Path, however, is only a short distance across the moor. There is no sign of Offa's Dyke itself (the eighth-century border ran along the Wye to the east), but the ridge forming the present-day England/Wales border provides fine scenic views.

A gentle descent to Llanthony concludes our walk. There are more memorable views to savour, including an impressive bird's-eye perspective of the abbey itself.

LLANTHONY, CWMYOY & HATTERRALL HILL

DISTANCE: 13.8KM/8.5MILES » **TOTAL ASCENT:** 533M/1,749FT » **START GR:** SO 289278 » **TIME:** ALLOW 4.5 HOURS **MAP:** OS EXPLORER OL13, BRECON BEACONS NATIONAL PARK EASTERN AREA, 1:25,000 » **REFRESHMENTS:** THE LLANTHONY PRIORY HOTEL AND THE HALF MOON HOTEL, LLANTHONY » **NAVIGATION:** GENERALLY EASY, BUT SOME PATHS INTERMITTENTLY WAYMARKED BETWEEN LLANTHONY AND CWMYOY, AND A SHORT SECTION OF UNDEFINED PATH ON HATTERRALL HILL.

LLANTHONY PRIORY PHOTO: ADAM LONG

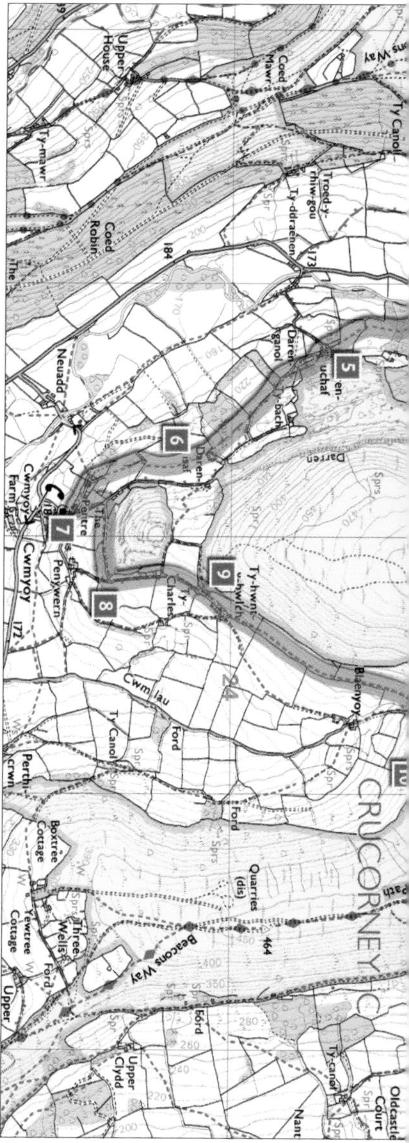

04 LLANTHONY, CWMYOY & HATTERRALL HILL

Directions – Llanthony, Cwmyoy & Hatterrall Hill

S Go back out through the car park entrance and **turn left** into Court Farm (there is no initial waymark but there is an obvious pony trekking sign). Keep **straight ahead** through the farmyard and climb gently along a track across fields. In the **fourth** field, **bear slightly left** to join a path along a ditch and fence (the walking is easier on the field side of the ditch, which can be crossed at the far end). Go over a stile and climb through woods on a narrow, overgrown path. At the top, cross another field towards a ruined farmstead.

2 **Turn right** by the ruins along the remains of a hollow lane hugging the contour of the mountain. The lane is overgrown in a number of places, but by deviating above or below as required, you can follow its line without difficulty for the next 2km or so.

3 At a further ruin, leave the lane by **bearing right**, between the buildings, then **left** along the top of a field. At the end of the field, **drop right** as far as a gate and ford on the left. Go through the gate and pass through the ruins of a sizable farm.

4 A grassy track slopes down from the ruin to the Honddu. Follow the river to a footbridge. **Ignore** the bridge and climb the stile ahead. Follow a clear track up a wooded slope to a field below a farm. **Turn left** along the fence in the waymarked direction and climb to a rough track along the bottom edge of the hill.

5 **Turn right** along the track, passing above the farm and left of a corrugated barn. Follow a grassy track above the next house, then **bear left** to cross the higher of two gates **on the right**. Join a grassy track, soon **bearing left** uphill. As you start to climb, **turn right** through a gateway and cross a field towards a house.

6 Cross the access track below the house and **bear slightly right**, aiming for a stile where the field boundary on the far side forms a reflex angle. In the next field, **bear right** along the fence, then keep **straight ahead** to a track in the bottom corner. Join a lane and continue to the north gate of Cwmyoy's 'crooked' church.

7 After viewing the church, retrace your steps and **turn right** onto a footpath signed *Graig*. Climb steeply on an enclosed path to a gate and information board. **Turn right** along the base of Graig, the rocky, jagged hill on your left.

8 At a junction, **turn left** onto a rough track and climb until a better track is met by an abandoned house. Keep **straight ahead** towards a farmhouse. **Ignore** the right turn through the farm and keep **straight ahead** into a field.

9 Follow a fence up the valley until just past Blaenyoy (the farm below). **Fork right** at an obvious divide in the path, then **swing right** to cross a ford at the head of the valley. Just past this point, **turn left**, following the grassy track from Blaenyoy up to the common. **Turn right** along the wall to a gate onto the hill.

10 Keep **straight ahead** up the hill on a clear turf path. The path becomes more vague, eventually petering out altogether. **Ignore** the right of way marked on OS maps and cross rough moor to the east for about 100m to intersect with Offa's Dyke Path.

11 **Turn left** and follow Offa's Dyke Path north along the ridge. Descend gently to a path crossroads signed *Llanthony* and *Longtown*. After admiring the views to the right, **turn left** and descend along a clear path for a little over 1.5km. At a junction of paths, **turn left** onto the path signed *Llanthony*.

12 Cross a field to a wood. On the far side, aim for the north end of the priory wall and **bear right**. **Turn left** along a gravel track and emerge near the car park entrance opposite Court Farm.

ENTRANCE TO THE VALE OF EWYAS FROM YSGYRYD FAWR PHOTO: ADAM LONG

TWMPA OR LORD HEREFORD'S KNOB FROM HAY BLUFF PHOTO: ADAM LONG

05 The Black Hill, Hay Bluff & Capel-y-ffin

18.4km/11.4miles

Ridge-top walking on the Wales/England border.

Black Hill picnic site » Black Hill (640m) » Hay Bluff (677m) » Gospel Pass » Darren Lwyd » Capel-y-ffin » Olchon Valley » Black Hill picnic site

Start

Free car park at Black Hill picnic site. This is off a minor road to the north-west of Llanveynoe. GR: SO 288328.

The Walk

For administrative convenience, the eastern boundary of the Brecon Beacons National Park coincides with the Wales-England border. However, the special qualities of the Black Mountains occur either side of the political divide. This route follows a line along the finest of Herefordshire's ridges, Crib y Garth or the Cat's Back, before crossing back into Wales near Hay Bluff.

We begin our walk from the Black Hill picnic site, heading straight up to a narrow, airy ridge between the Olchon and Monnow valleys. Continuing north-west from the Black Hill trig point, we round the top of the Olchon Valley to meet up with Offa's Dyke Path. A short distance to the north, Hay Bluff marks the north end of the Hatterrall ridge and offers far-reaching views across the Wye Valley.

Further big climbs can be avoided by returning south along Offa's Dyke Path; the full route continues on to Capel-y-ffin ('chapel of the border') via Gospel Pass and the Darren Lwyd escarpment. After visiting the famous chapel (described by Victorian diarist, Francis Kilvey, as 'squatting like a stout grey owl'), we follow an ancient trackway down the valley to 'The Vision Farm', renamed in 1880 following reputed sightings of the Virgin Mary. Spiritual assistance may now be required: the climb across the ridge to the Olchon Valley is the toughest of the day.

The Olchon Valley is a hidden gem, largely ignored because of its location outside the National Park and its serene peace is ample reward for the day's efforts. One final climb takes us back to the Black Hill picnic site.

THE BLACK HILL, HAY BLUFF & CAPEL-Y-FFIN

DISTANCE: 18.4KM/11.4MILES » **TOTAL ASCENT:** 801M/2,628FT » **START GR:** SO 288328 » **TIME:** ALLOW 6.5 HOURS **MAP:** OS EXPLORER OL13, BRECON BEACONS NATIONAL PARK EASTERN AREA, 1:25,000 » **REFRESHMENTS:** NONE ON ROUTE; NEAREST PUBS ARE THE CROWN INN, LONGTOWN, AND THE CORNEWALL ARMS, CLODOCK » **NAVIGATION:** EASY EXCEPT FOR INDISTINCT PATH BETWEEN GOSPEL PASS AND DARREN LWYD.

Darren Lwyd
Tarren yr Esgob
Blaen-bwch
Standing Stone
Nant Bwch
Rain Gauge
Talsarn
Waun-goch
Boxbush
The Grange
The Monastery
Mon
Pen-y-maes
Capel-y-ffin
Chapel Farm
Y Fferm
Blaenau
Trwyn-tal
Capel y Ffin
Afon Honddu
Ford
Waun-rydd
Tyn-y-drain
Nant Hywel
Sheepfold
Cwm Brychen
Maes-y-ffin
Ty-canol
Ty-Shores
Ty'r-onen
Nant Ffin
The Vision Farm
Nant Vision
Waterfalls
Offa's Dyke Path
Pile of Stones
Auburys
Firs Farm
The Place
Town House
Fords
Olchon Court
Hillside
Olchon
5
6
7
8
9
10
31

05 THE BLACK HILL, HAY BLUFF & CAPEL-Y-FFIN

Directions – The Black Hill, Hay Bluff & Capel-y-ffin

S Cross the stile at the back of the car park and head straight up the hill. The initial ascent is steep, but the gradient soon eases on a narrow, airy ridge between the Monnow and Olchon valleys. Continue on an obvious path, the ridge widening as you approach Black Hill.

2 **Bear left** on a well-worn path from the trig point and follow this north-west past the head of the Olchon Valley. Offa's Dyke Path is met near a fork. **Ignore** the official route to the right and keep **straight ahead** onto a gravel path. Follow the peaty ridge north-west to the trig point on Hay Bluff.

SC ***SC**: To shorten the route and avoid further big climbs, retrace your steps and continue south along Offa's Dyke Path. Climb briefly to the trail high point, then descend gradually for about 3km. Rejoin the main route at the end of point **8**, about 400m past the top of a second slight rise, where a marker stone indicates a path crossroads between Capel-y-ffin and the Olchon Valley.

3 **Turn left** onto the gravel path along the Black Mountains' northern escarpment. **Ignore** a sharp right turn down the slope and keep **straight ahead** on the grassy escarpment path. Descend steeply to the road at Gospel Pass.

4 Cross the road and keep **straight ahead** up the slope. Where a path from a car park joins from the left, keep **straight ahead** onto a poorly defined path climbing diagonally across the slope to the south. The path is quite vague, but **ignore** any trails heading directly up the slope on the right. Keep pressing ahead until you emerge on a narrow 'trod' along an exhilarating escarpment edge.

5 As the ridge narrows, keep **straight ahead** onto a larger path running south from Lord Hereford's Knob. Continue along the ever-narrowing ridge, descending past one cairn, then shortly meeting another.

6 Drop steeply, **swinging sharply left** then **right**. Keep **straight ahead** across a level path crossroads, then **bear left** down a rough track alongside a fence. Leave the common and pass between houses. Keep **straight ahead** across a stile and descend through a field to a road. Watching out for traffic, **turn right** along the lane for about 250m to a telephone box and chapel (Capel-y-ffin).

7 **Turn left** onto a track in front of the chapel. A short distance ahead, pass another chapel (this time Baptist) and **swing right**. Continue past a house onto a hollow lane above Afon Honddu, then onto a field path. Cross a stone stile and follow the **left edge** of two fields to the corner of a sunken track. Keep **straight ahead**.

8 Join a tarmac lane at Ty'r-onen and descend gently through two gateways. After the second, **turn left** at a footpath signed *Offa's Dyke*. Follow clear markers to the **right**, past The Vision Farm, then head **straight up** to the common and **turn right** along its bottom edge. After a short level section, **climb steeply left**. As the gradient eases, **ignore** a left fork (which meets Offa's Dyke Path too far north), and **fork right** across the headwaters of Nant Vision. Emerge on Offa's Dyke Path by a marker stone with a path to the *Olchon Valley* signed directly ahead.

9 Descend **diagonally left**, then **diagonally right**. Keep **straight ahead** at a waymarked fork, then **straight ahead** again at a path crossroads. Aim towards a wooded area in the bottom corner of the common. Pass through a kissing gate and follow a fence to a second kissing gate. **Bear left** along the line of a sunken grassy track and descend to a lane. **Turn left** to a T-junction, then **left** again.

10 Shortly, **turn right** over a stile into a field. Follow the edge of the field downhill, then **bear left** to a footbridge over the Olchon Brook. **Bear right** and climb along the edge of a field. Where directed, **bear right** again, towards Blackhill Farm. Keep **straight ahead** past the farm onto a sunken path and climb through woodland close to a stream. **Turn left** at a lane, then shortly **right**. Follow the access road back up the hill to the Black Hill picnic site.

Y GRIB AND PENGENFFORD. PHOTO: ADAM LONG

06 Castell Dinas & Rhos Dirion

16.5km/10.3miles

Above and below the Black Mountains' northern escarpment.

Dragons Back, Pengenffordd » Rhos Dirion (713m) » Y Grîb » Castell Dinas (450m) » Dragons Back pub, Pengenffordd

Start

Dragons Back pub car park in Pengenffordd. GR: SO 173296.

The Walk

This memorable circuit explores both top and base of the Black Mountains' impressive north-facing escarpment. Saving the best for last, we finish with a dramatic traverse of the long, slender ridge of Y Grîb, and a walk through the crumbling ramparts of the highest stone castle in Wales.

We begin with a long trek around the escarpment base, our route dipping in and out of the numerous narrow valleys channelling water down the Black Mountains' steep northern slopes. Gradually gaining height, we approach Rhiw Wen, an ancient mountain roadway, and begin climbing in earnest. As we ascend, far-reaching views open out across the Wye Valley towards the Radnorshire hills.

Our return leg follows the high escarpment edge, which narrows to the west into the slender grassy ridge of Y Grîb. The airy traverse of this ridge is a particularly delightful section of the walk. The hard work is not over yet, however, as once off the ridge we are faced with a short, stiff pull up to the crumbling castle ramparts of Castell Dinas – but this is a climb well worth the effort. At 450m, the castle was the highest stone-built fortification in Wales and provides splendid views along the valley either side of the Rhiangoll pass. A steep descent through fields takes us swiftly back to the Dragons Back pub.

CASTELL DINAS & RHOS DIRION

DISTANCE: 16.5KM/10.3MILES » **TOTAL ASCENT:** 585M/1,919FT » **START GR:** SO 173296 » **TIME:** ALLOW 5.5 HOURS
MAP: OS EXPLORER OL13, BRECON BEACONS NATIONAL PARK EASTERN AREA, 1:25,000 » **REFRESHMENTS:** DRAGONS BACK PUB, PENGENFFORDD (FRIDAY NIGHTS AND SATURDAYS ONLY); NEAREST OTHER PUB IS THE FARMERS ARMS, CWMDU
NAVIGATION: STRAIGHTFORWARD WALK IN FINE WEATHER.

TWMPA FROM HAY BLUFF PHOTO: ADAM LONG

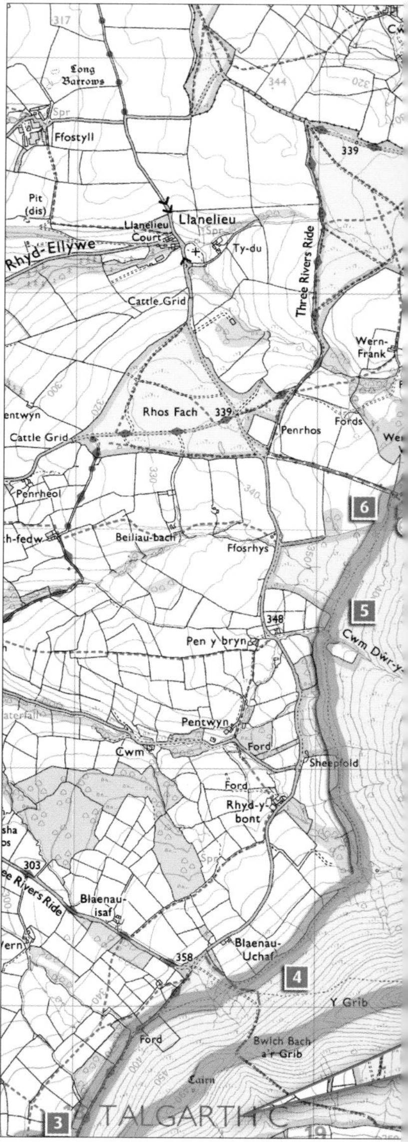

06 CASTELL DINAS & RHOS DIRION

Directions – Castell Dinas & Rhos Dirion

S Descend steps at the top end of the pub car park. **Turn right** along an enclosed track, then immediately **left** over a stile into a field. Walk down the field, cross a stream, and follow a field boundary steeply uphill. In the next field, **ignore** the path ahead towards Castell Dinas and **turn left** over a stile.

2 **Bear slightly right** across the field. Keep **straight ahead** in the next field to a stile onto a lane. **Turn right** towards a farm, then **bear right** onto a track. After a sharp right-hand bend, climb steeply to open common in the col between Castell Dinas and Y Grîb.

3 **Bear left** on obvious track along the base of the common. Do not descend, but **bear right** onto a path to maintain height. Rejoin the common boundary further along the hill.

4 On approaching Cwm y Nant, **bear right**, away from the common edge, and cross a number of small streams funnelling into the valley. Cross the stony bed of the main stream, then **bear left** to rejoin a path above the common boundary. Where the boundary fence drops away, keep **straight ahead**. Pass below an enclosed field and cross a stream.

5 Briefly rejoin the common edge, which again drops left. Keep **straight ahead** across an area with no obvious route (if boggy, drier ground can be found higher up the slope). Pass through gorse bushes to a small wooden gate in a fence.

SC ***SC**: For a much shorter walk, **turn right** in front of the fence and follow the Rhiw Cwnstab bridleway to the top of the escarpment. Rejoin the main route towards the end of point **8**.

6 Pass through the fence and follow the path along the edge of Wern Frank Wood. Cross the stream in Cwm Cwnstab and keep **straight ahead** across another area of open ground where the common boundary drops away. Rejoin the boundary along the edge of deciduous woodland. Where the trees on the left are replaced by open fields, **bear right** towards the top corner of a fence.

CONTINUES ON PAGE 45

07 THE LLANBEDR HORSESHOE

GRWYNE FECHAN VALLEY PHOTO: TRACY BURTON

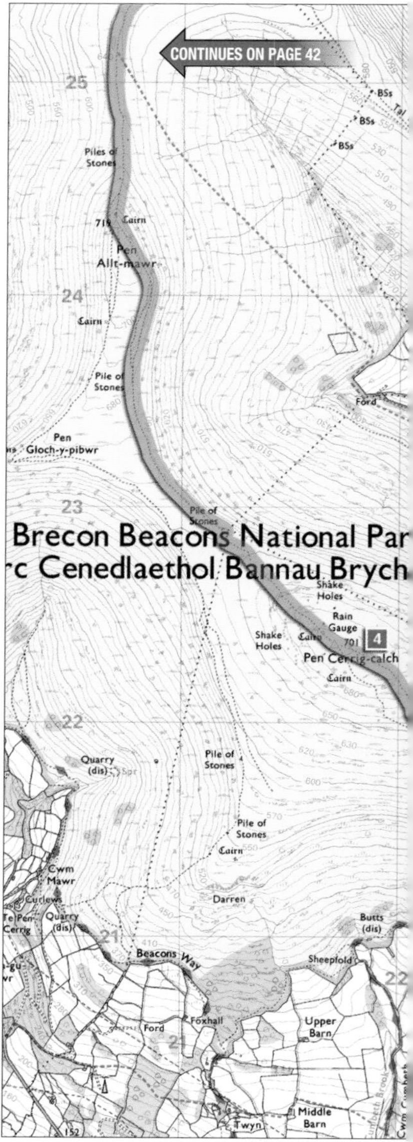

CONTINUES ON PAGE 42

07 THE LLANBEDR HORSESHOE

Directions – The Llanbedr Horseshoe

S Follow the lane north from the lay-by, passing a large farmhouse on the right. Shortly, **turn left** up the concrete access track to Perth-y-pia, signed *Table Mountain*. Climb steeply to the stone farmhouse, then keep **straight ahead** across a grassy area to the right of the building and cross a stile into a field. Follow the field boundary uphill to a wooden gate onto the common.

2 Continue uphill between the common boundary and a stream. **Turn left** along the boundary wall, then immediately **fork right** to climb diagonally across the hill. Shortly, **swing right**, climbing diagonally in the opposite direction. When level with the boundary corner below, **turn left** and climb onto the flat-topped summit of Table Mountain.

3 Locate a path near the north end of the summit and descend into a dip. Keep **straight ahead** on an obvious ascending path, **swinging right** then **left** for the easiest route. The path reaches a wide plateau, but continues to climb steadily. Pass through outcrops of limestone to the summit of Pen Cerrig-calch.

4 Continue north-west past the trig point and drop to an escarpment edge overlooking Cwm Banw. Follow the escarpment north to Pen Allt-mawr (there is a large shelter cairn on the summit if required). After a short, steep descent, **bear right** along the ridge, passing around the head of Cwm Banw to Pen Twyn Glas. **Fork to the left** of the grassy summit and continue north along a wide ridge towards Mynydd Llysiau.

5 Drop steeply to a saddle between Mynydd Llysiau and Pen Trumau; a cairn marks the junction of a number of bridleways. Keep **straight ahead** and climb steeply onto the flatter ground of Pen Trumau. The path forks, both branches soon rejoining. **Curve right** above the headwaters of the Grwyne Fechan to a final steep pull onto the boggy plateau of Waun Fach. Unless exceptionally dry, the concrete block marking the summit is likely to stand in a morass of wet peat.

6 **Bear right** from Waun Fach, heading roughly south-east across the boggy plateau. There is no obvious path at first, but as the ridge narrows, pick up a wide grassy path to Pen y Gadair Fawr. Keep **straight ahead** across the summit and along the ridge to the right of Mynydd Du Forest. Large areas of this plantation have been cleared, but the former forest edge is still quite clear. Cross Pen Twyn Mawr and join a more defined track running through an area of heather and sandy soil.

7 **Fork right** at the end of the forest to pass below and to the right of Crug Mawr. (**Alternatively, fork left** for the summit, then **right** to return to the main route.) Join the Beacons Way and cruise easily above Cwm Milaid. Keep to the main path, passing **to the right** of higher ground, and descend to a dry-stone wall.

8 Keep **straight ahead** where the wall turns left and descend more steeply. **Swing left** by two hawthorn trees, rejoining the common boundary lower down the hill. Descend to the bottom corner of the common and continue **ahead** through a metal gate. Follow a sunken track below trees for about 500m.

9 **Turn right** at a stile and drop down a steep bank to a track behind a house. **Turn right** into a field, then **bear left**, down to a stile in the bottom corner. **Bear slightly left** in the next field, aiming for a stile onto a lane. Cross the road and continue along a field edge to a stile into woods. Follow a zigzagging path down a steep wooded slope to the river below.

10 Cross a stone bridge over the Grwyne Fechan and follow a stony track uphill into Llanbedr. Pass the church and Red Lion pub and take the road **straight ahead** through the village. Climb gently for about 600m to return to your starting point.

VIEW SOUTH OVER WAUN FACH FROM THE AIR PHOTO: ADRIAN LONG

THE USK VALLEY FROM ALLT YR ESGAIR PHOTO: TRACY BURTON

08 The Llangors Loop

17.8km/11.1miles

A circuit round Llangors Lake via Allt yr Esgair and Mynydd Llangorse.

Llangors Common » Allt yr Esgair (393m) » Bwlch » Mynydd Llangorse (515m) » Llangors » Llangors Common

Start

Car park adjacent to public toilets on Llangors Common. GR: SO 128272.

The Walk

Like many geographical features in the Black Mountains, Llangors Lake is the product of glacial action during the last Ice Age. As the ice melted, moraine deposits trapped water in the bowl-shaped valley, creating a wide, shallow lake. Now much smaller, the lake is still the largest natural body of water in South Wales and is rich in flora and fauna, particularly bird life. The paths followed on this walk are some distance from the lake itself, but offer frequent glimpses of its shimmering waters.

We begin a short distance from the lake, on Llangors Common (a visit to the shore either before or after the walk is a must). A low-lying path prone to flooding takes us around the lake's western shore to Llangasty, where a beautifully constructed bird hide presents an opportunity for wildlife spotting. The lake is often hidden by vegetation on this section of the walk, but there are splendid views of the surrounding mountains.

Our next objective, the wooded ridge of Allt yr Esgair, is a pure delight, with panoramic views complemented in May and June by a wild profusion of colourful flowers. Traces of past human settlement on the ridge are also visible, including a Bronze Age burial cairn, Iron Age hill fort and Roman road.

After descending into Bwlch (drinks and snacks available in the village shop), we turn northwards onto the long, heathery ridge leading to Mynydd Llangorse. Beyond the summit, a clear grassy path drops to a road pass below Mynydd Troed. If feeling fit, we may wish to take the steep path to the top, but this is purely optional! The main route follows the lane downhill into Llangors, a picturesque village with two tempting pubs. A short stroll across fields and we are back on the common.

THE LLANGORS LOOP

DISTANCE: 17.8KM/11.1MILES » **TOTAL ASCENT:** 558M/1,831FT » **START GR:** SO 128272 » **TIME:** ALLOW 5.5 HOURS **MAP:** OS EXPLORER OL13, BRECON BEACONS NATIONAL PARK EASTERN AREA, 1:25,000 » **REFRESHMENTS:** GATE SHOP, BWLCH; THE CASTLE INN, THE RED LION, AND THE LAKESIDE RESTAURANT, LLANGORS » **NAVIGATION:** STRAIGHTFORWARD IN FINE WEATHER.

Sewage Works
Ashford
Llansantffraed
Allt
Rock Wood
Enclosure
Paragon Tower
Allt House
Allt yr Esgair
The Elms
Sunnybank
Talybryn Lodge
Tal-y-bryn
Quarry (dis)
Buckland Farm
Pentremelin
Y Coed
Penparc
ROMAN ROAD
A 40
Glanpant
Middlewood Farm
Middle Wood Cottage
Three Rivers Ride
Trebinshwn Farm
Trebinshwn Cottage
Trebinshwn
Afon Llynfi
Point Cottage
Neuadd Farm
Danyrallt
Cathedine Common
Lower Cathedine
Wern-ddu
Pasturefields
Llanfellte
5
Castle Wood
Castell Blaenllynfi (remains of)
Pendre
B 4560
Bwlch
Quarries (dis)
6
Bwlch Wood
Cathedine Hill
Heol-las Farm
Penllyn
The Old Rectory
Nant-y-felin-isaf
Nant-y-felin-uchaf
Ford
Upper Cathedine
Treholford Wood
Treholford
Penyrheol
15
Cwm Nant-y-felin
Dingle Wood
Reservoir
Pen-yr-heol-las
Quarries (dis)
Cairn
Quarry (dis)
25
Maesclythan Wood
Beacons Way
7
Cefn Moel
Burnt Mound
Mound
Pen-y-graig
Clwydygraig
Blaen-y-cwm-isaf
Cilfaenor
Pen-yr-heol
The Crindau
Gwndwn
Talsarn
Neuadd-fry
Penlan
Ffynnon-las
Tremynydd
Cattle Grid
Tre-graig
Tynmawr
Tyle
Maes-llechau
Pen-y-gaer ROMAN FORT
Ewyn Brook

08 THE LLANGORS LOOP

Directions – The Llangors Loop

S From the public toilets, **turn right** onto the road, then immediately **left** onto a grassy path across the common. Keep **straight ahead** to a footbridge over Afon Llynfi. **Bear left** across a field to a gate, then keep **straight ahead** on an obvious path through two more fields.

2 Pass through a band of trees, **curving left** as you do so. Continue onto a wide, grassy path towards a wooden gate. Keep **straight ahead** at a waymark post and cross two more fields to a junction with a gravel vehicle track on the edge of woodland. The main route **turns right**, away from the lake, but it is worth descending first to the bird hide on the left. There are good views from here across the lake.

3 Follow the track across a field and past *Tymawr Farm*. **Swing left** up the access drive to a T-junction with a lane and **turn right**. Just before *Llangasty Village Hall*, **turn left** onto a bridleway.

4 Climb between high hedges to a junction of paths and **turn left**. Climb steadily along Allt yr Esgair, a beautiful ridge with fantastic panoramic views. Follow the path along the ridge and descend to run alongside a dry-stone wall. Lower down, the path is enclosed between high hedges and may be muddy. Emerge on the corner of a lane and keep **straight ahead** downhill to a T-junction with the A40.

5 **Turn left** along the main road into Bwlch (there is no pavement at first, but one soon appears on the left). After passing *Gate Shop* (teas, coffees and sandwiches), watch out for a stile **on the left** where the houses end. Follow a path uphill and **to the right**, crossing a field. **Pass to the left** of a garden wall to a stile onto a lane.

6 **Turn left** and follow the lane uphill. At a *Beacons Way* marker, **turn left** onto a track and climb steeply. Keep **straight ahead** onto open common and continue climbing. Where the gradient eases, **continue ahead**, following a track by a fence and wall along the crest of the ridge.

7 At a junction of bridleways, keep **straight ahead** towards Mynydd Llangorse. **Fork left** onto a smaller path below the summit and climb past a trig point. The mountain's true summit lies some 600m north of the trig point and is marked by a small pile of stones to the right of the track.

8 The steep flanks of Mynydd Troed are now clearly visible. Keep **straight ahead** down a narrowing ridge and drop to a road pass between the two summits. **Turn left** down the hill and follow this lane for almost 3km to a T-junction with the main road through Llangors.

OR If you wish to 'bag' Mynydd Troed, cross the road and keep **straight ahead** up the steep slope. Climb hard, then **bear right** onto a grassy track for the final pull to the summit. Return the same way and follow the lane downhill to Llangors.

9 **Turn right** through Llangors, passing the Castle Inn. Just after the pub, **turn left** along a narrow passage leading to a field. Follow the clear waymarks across several fields back to your starting point on Llangors Common.

LLANGORS LAKE PHOTO: ADAM LONG

SECTION 2

The Brecon Beacons, Mynydd Llangatwg & Mynydd Llangynidr

This section contains two distinct areas, both bordered to the north by the River Usk's green valley. The Brecon Beacons are a line of popular peaks to the south of Brecon whose name is now frequently used to refer to the National Park as a whole. The Brecon Beacons proper form a long ridge containing the park's two highest peaks, Corn Du (873m) and Pen y Fan (886m). East of these summits, Mynydd Llangatwg and Mynydd Llangynidr make up one wide expanse of untamed upland, riddled with shake holes and rocky outcrops. Clydach Gorge marks the southeastern border of this moorland, while spectacular limestone cliffs form its eastern edge above Crickhowell.

CRIBYN PHOTO: ADAM LONG

CRIBYN FROM PEN Y FAN PHOTO: ADAM LONG

CRAIG Y CILAU PHOTO: ADAM LONG

09 Llangattock & Craig y Cilau

15.6km/9.7miles

Spectacular limestone cliffs above the Usk Valley.

Llangattock » Dardy » Ffawyddog » Cwm Onnau » Craig y Cilau » Pant-y-rhiw » Llangattock

Start

Free car park at the end of Church View (opposite the church) in Llangattock. GR: SO 210178.

The Walk

Llangattock is a pretty village just across the River Usk from Crickhowell. Starting from its centre, this walk explores part of the Usk Valley Walk (including a short section along the Monmouthshire & Brecon Canal) and the impressive natural amphitheatre formed by the cliffs of Craig y Cilau.

Our walk begins from St Catwg's Church in Llangattock. After a short section along the Monmouthshire & Brecon Canal, we climb on the Usk Valley Walk to join a field path contouring across the valley slope. The path connects a number of abandoned farms and provides excellent views.

After a further climb, we leave the Usk Valley Walk and continue upwards to the edge of a wide expanse of open moorland. Never straying far from the common boundary, we follow a rough path across the headwaters of Nant Onneu and climb to an unfenced mountain road.

A two-kilometre road walk leads to Craig y Cilau National Nature Reserve, an area of spectacular limestone cliffs that forms the highlight of the walk. The cliffs were extensively quarried in the nineteenth century and a former tramroad provides easy level walking along their base. On the way, we may want to stop and explore the entrance to Eglwys Faen ('stone church'), the most accessible of the many caves that pockmark the Craig y Cilau escarpment. Other caves, such as Agen Allwedd and Daren Cilau, provide access to an extensive system of underground passages extending far below the mountain. The entranceways to these latter two caves are locked, with access available to experienced cavers only.

Soon after reaching the road at Pant-y-rhiw, we begin a steep descent along a rough, stony track, which may be wet after rain. Once down, easy field paths take us back to Llangattock.

LLANGATTOCK & CRAIG Y CILAU

DISTANCE: 15.6KM/9.7MILES » **TOTAL ASCENT:** 468M/1,535FT » **START GR:** SO 210178 » **TIME:** ALLOW 5 HOURS
MAP: OS EXPLORER OL13, BRECON BEACONS NATIONAL PARK EASTERN AREA, 1:25,000 » **REFRESHMENTS:** NONE ON ROUTE, BUT PLENTY OF CHOICE ACROSS THE RIVER IN CRICKHOWELL » **NAVIGATION:** NO MAJOR PROBLEMS IN GOOD VISIBILITY.

CHURCH AT LLANGATTOCK PHOTO: ADAM LONG

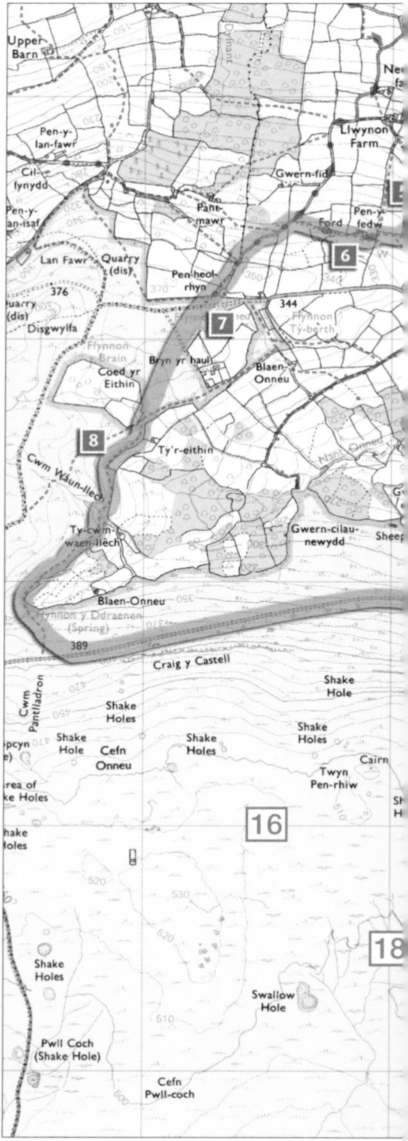

09 LLANGATTOCK & CRAIG Y CILAU

Directions – Llangattock & Craig y Cilau

S Walk back along Church View to a T-junction and **turn left**. Just after the Old Rectory Hotel, **bear right** through a kissing gate and climb diagonally across a field to the towpath of the Monmouthshire & Brecon Canal.

2 **Turn right** onto the towpath, passing below a road at Bridge *118*. At Bridge *119*, leave the canal by crossing the bridge and **bearing left** onto a stony bridleway marked *Usk Valley Walk*. Climb steeply through woodland to a junction of tracks and **turn left** in the direction of a bridleway arrow. Follow the bridleway to a lane and keep **straight ahead** to a T-junction by the Old Sunday School.

3 **Turn right** along the lane. At a left-hand bend, keep **straight ahead**, crossing a stile into a field. Follow the waymarked path across fields to a junction with a grassy track by a derelict farm. Keep **straight ahead** between the buildings and go through a metal gate into a field.

4 Follow the right edge of a field to a second field. Keep **straight ahead** towards a gate into a third field, then **bear left** uphill towards a stone barn. Pass to the left of the barn, then **bear left** across a stile into woodland. Follow a path through trees and exit the wood with another abandoned farm just ahead.

5 **Turn sharp left** on a grassy track along the woodland boundary. Climb steeply into a narrow strip of field and **swing right** to a field gate. Enter another steeply sloping field, crossing it diagonally to a stile in the top fence. **Bear right**, across the corner of a field, to another stile. Keep **straight ahead** towards an abandoned farm.

6 Join a track to the left of the farm and descend gently across fields to a junction with an enclosed track. **Turn left** and climb steeply. Emerge onto open common near a house and keep **straight ahead** to a road.

7 Cross the road and continue southwest, parallel to the common boundary on the left. **Turn left** at a gravel track towards the corner of a dry-stone wall. **Bear right** here, aiming for a narrow strip of common between enclosed fields. **Fork left** in the gap, following the common boundary past another abandoned farm.

8 Follow a rough but clear path through Cwm Waun-llech, then across the upper reaches of Nant Onneu. Once across the stream, **bear left** and climb to a two-way road. **Turn left** and follow the grass verge for close to 2km (beware of fast-moving traffic). With a cattle grid ahead, **turn right** onto a gravel vehicle track.

9 **Ignore** the continuation of the track through a gate and **turn right** along a fence. Descend past an information board for *Craig y Cilau National Nature Reserve* and **bear to the right** of a flat, marshy area. At a waymark post just beyond the marsh, **fork right** in the direction of a white arrow.

10 Follow a narrow, undulating path up to the grassy remains of a former tramroad. **Turn left** and follow the level path of the tramway along the base of the Craig y Cilau escarpment. About 250m further on, where the path begins to curve left, **detour right** up a narrow, zigzagging path to Eglwys Faen, a cave whose wide entrance can be explored with care. Rejoin the tramway.

11 The tramway continues for over 1km. Join a track by a stone house and continue **ahead** onto a lane. After about 400m, **turn left** down an access lane marked *Laswern-fawr*. Continue past the house onto an enclosed track and **swing left** down the slope on a rough, stony track. About 500m below a derelict chapel, **swing sharp left** to a house, then **right** to a lane. **Bear left** down the lane to a sharp left-hand bend and keep **straight ahead** over a stile.

12 Follow the right edge of the field to a further stile. Keep **straight ahead** along a clear path in the next field to a stone bridge over the Monmouthshire & Brecon Canal. Cross the canal and continue along a track with a fence to your right. Where the track swings left to a farm, keep **straight ahead** over a stile into woods. Descend through a narrow strip of woodland and emerge in a large field.

13 Strike out across the field, aiming for the far end of a hedge bordering a campsite to your left. Go through a kissing gate onto an access track and **bear right**, immediately passing round a left-hand bend. Join a residential road in Llangynidr and continue to a T-junction opposite the (currently closed) Horseshoe Inn. **Turn left**, then **right**, following a narrow village street to St Catwg's Church and the car park.

TALYBONT RESERVOIR AND GLYN COLLWN PHOTO: TRACY BURTON

10 Cwm Cleisfer & Tor y Foel

21.1km/13.1miles

Industrial history in a wild mountain landscape.

Llangynidr » Cwm Cleisfer » Ogof Fawr (Chartist Cave) » Dyffryn Crawnon » Pen Rhiw-calch » Tor y Foel (551m) » Llangynidr

Start

Free car park off the B4558 in Llangynidr. Public conveniences opposite. GR: SO 155196.

The Walk

Today the preserve of leisure craft and walkers, the peaceful waters of the Monmouthshire & Brecon Canal were once part of a busy transport network linking rural and industrial Wales. One of the most important links in this network was the Brinore Tramroad, which connected the iron works and limestone quarries of Tredegar and Trefil with the canal at Talybont-on-Usk. The section around the precipitous slopes of Dyffryn Crawnon is truly spectacular and is now a popular walking trail.

We begin, however, on the far side of the mountain from the Brinore Tramroad, in Llangynidr. Heading up the narrow valley of Cwm Cleisfer, we pick up a tumbling mountain stream and follow it to its source on the wild moorland of Mynydd Llangynidr. This is a delightful stretch of walk along a beautiful valley, though the going can be difficult in places. Moorland paths take us past Ogof Fawr or the Chartist Cave, an isolated spot reputed to have been used by Tredegar Chartists in the 1830s as a hiding place for pikes and other weapons.

Heading west, we pick up the Brinore Tramroad north of Trefil and follow it across the spectacular slopes above Dyffryn Crawnon. The tramroad continues into Glyn Collwn (there are lovely views of Talybont Reservoir below), but we turn right, along the ridge separating the two valleys, to climb Tor y Foel, a modest summit with expansive views. Once over the top, a long descent takes us down to the Monmouthshire & Brecon Canal on the western edge of Llangynidr. It is now a gentle stroll back to our starting point, mainly along the towpath of this lovely waterway.

CWM CLEISFER & TOR Y FOEL

DISTANCE: 21.1KM/13.1MILES » **TOTAL ASCENT:** 793M/2,602FT » **START GR:** SO 155196 » **TIME:** ALLOW 7 HOURS **MAP:** OS EXPLORER OL13, BRECON BEACONS NATIONAL PARK EASTERN AREA, 1:25,000 & OS EXPLORER OL12, BRECON BEACONS NATIONAL PARK WESTERN AREA, 1:25,000 » **REFRESHMENTS:** THE RED LION AND THE COACH & HORSES, LLANGYNIDR » **NAVIGATION:** THE SECTION ACROSS MYNYDD LLANGYNIDR IS NOT RECOMMENDED IN POOR VISIBILITY.

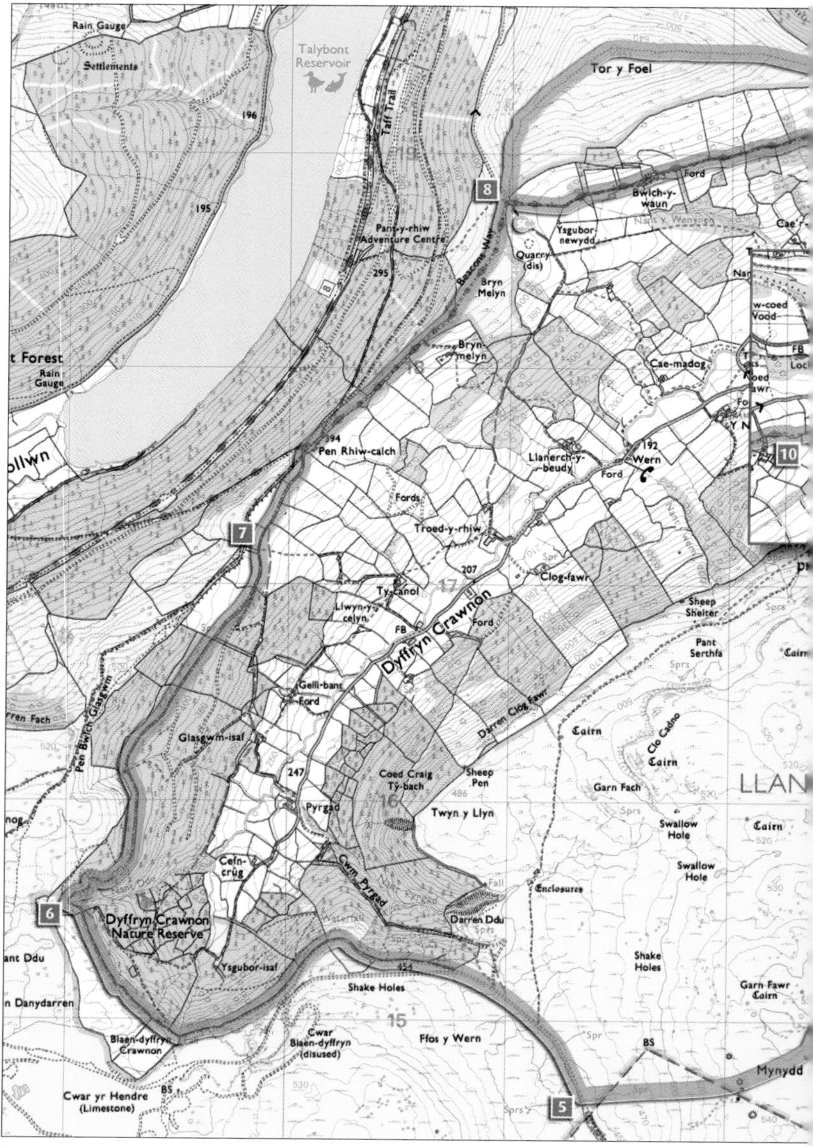

Rain Gauge
Settlements
Talybont Reservoir
Tor y Foel
196
195
Taff Trail
Pant-y-rhiw Adventure Centre
295
Beacons Way
Ford
Bwlch-y-waun
Nant y Wenynen
Ysgubor-newydd
Quarry (dis)
Bryn Melyn
Bryn-melyn
Cae-madog
Rain Gauge
394
Pen Rhiw-calch
Llanerch-y-beudy
192
Wern
Ford
Fords
Troed-y-rhiw
207
Clog-fawr
Ty-canol
Llwyn-y-celyn
FB
Dyffryn Crawnon
Ford
Sheep Shelter
Pant Serthfa
Gelli-bant
Ford
Darren Clog Fawr
Cairn
Clo Cadno
Cairn
Glasgwm-isaf
Pen Bwlch Glasgwm
247
Coed Craig Tŷ-bach
Sheep Pen
486
Garn Fach
Pyrgad
Twyn y Llyn
Swallow Hole
Cairn
Swallow Hole
Cefn-crûg
Cwm Pyrgad
Enclosures
Dyffryn Crawnon Nature Reserve
Darren Ddu
Waterfall
Ysgubor-isaf
454
Shake Holes
Shake Holes
Garn Fawr Cairn
n Danydarren
15
Blaen-dyffryn Crawnon
Cwar Blaen-dyffryn (disused)
Ffos y Wern
BS
Mynydd
Cwar yr Hendre (Limestone)
BS
530
5
6
7
8
10

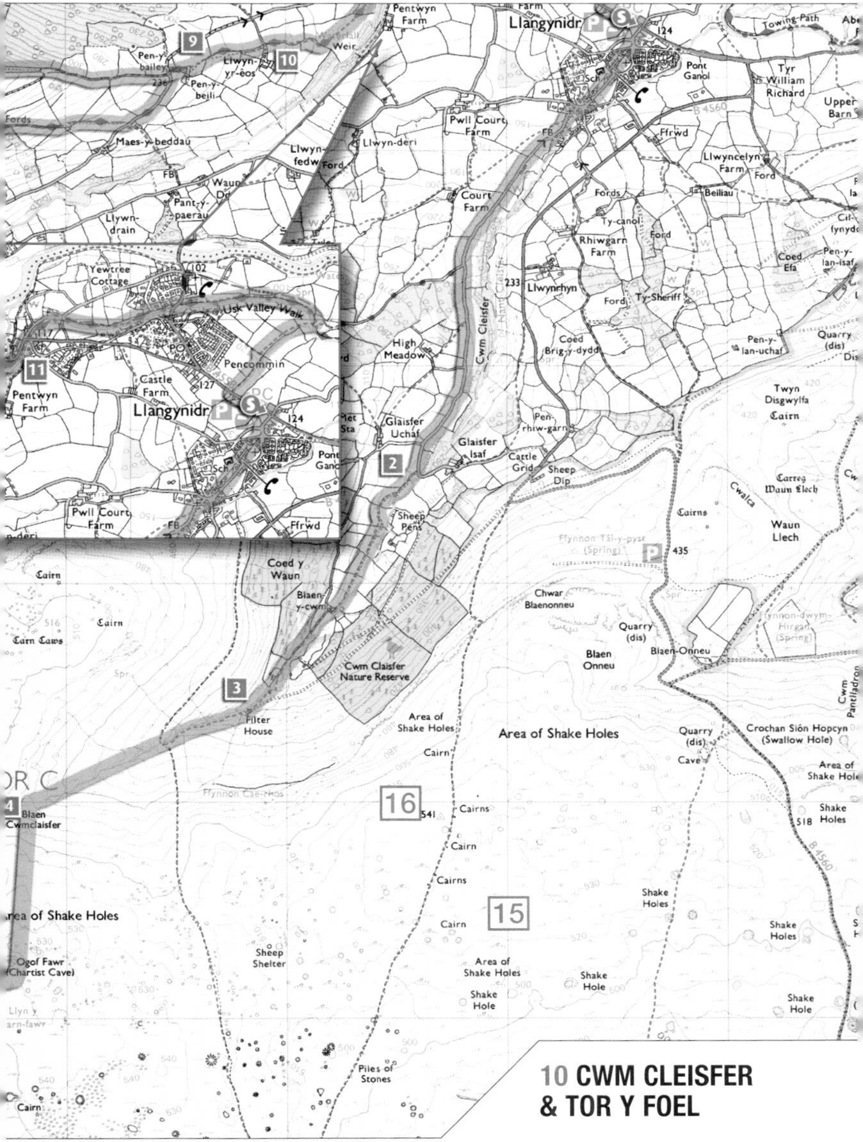

10 CWM CLEISFER & TOR Y FOEL

Directions – Cwm Cleisfer & Tor y Foel

S Walk to the far end of the car park and go through a gate. **Turn right** along a road as far as a stone stile just before the Red Lion. **Turn right** over the stile and follow a tarmac path through a graveyard and past the village church. Go through the main gate and keep **straight ahead** up the road. Where the road bears right, **turn left** at the second of two closely spaced turnings (Glaisfer Road). Pass between a chapel and graveyard and follow the narrow lane up Cwm Cleisfer for a little under 2km.

2 About 100m after the turn-off for Glaisfer Uchaf, the road swings sharply left across Nant Cleisfer. Just before the bridge, **bear right** through a metal gate and continue up the valley on a gravel track. After a short wooded section, the track crosses a number of small fields, eventually dwindling away. Keep **straight ahead** through metal gates, then **aim right** of a stone barn and join a rough track along a dry-stone wall. The track becomes narrower after a stile and runs closer to the stream.

3 Cross a forestry track and follow the right bank of the stream past an ugly red-brick building. Pick your way carefully along a faint, narrow trail, passing a number of small waterfalls. Shortly, you will need to **clamber right**, higher up the bank, to continue. At the next significant waterfall, **cross to the opposite bank**, then follow whichever bank is easier. The river source is reached by a jumble of rocks surrounding an isolated hawthorn tree.

4 **Bear left** from the source onto a faint path heading south. At a T-junction with a wider grassy path, **turn right** and pass the entrance to Ogof Fawr (or the 'Chartist Cave'). Where the main path bears left, keep **straight ahead** onto one of the smaller paths descending to the Trefil road. The path splits into a number of minor trails: aim for where a pile of boulders marks a small parking area.

5 **Turn right** along the road, which soon bears left. At the corner of a conifer plantation, **fork right** onto a gravel bridleway along the forest edge (part of the Brinore Tramroad). Where the gravel track bears left, away from the forest, keep **straight ahead** onto a grassy track. Follow the top line of trees around the head of Dyffryn Crawnon.

6 Cross a stream by a footbridge and enter a narrow, thickly wooded section where the path of the tramroad has been carved into a near-vertical slope. Damp below the trees makes mud likely throughout the year, and care should be taken where the edge

of the track has eroded to create precipitous drops. Eventually, the trees open out and the valley below is visible once more.

7 Keep **straight ahead** onto a gravel track ascending from the right. At a viewpoint and junction of tracks, **ignore** the continuation of the tramroad into Glyn Collwn and **turn right** onto a clear gravel track. Climb along the ridge between the two valleys, admiring excellent views of Talybont Reservor. Where the track divides, **fork right** along an ascending track marked *Beacons Way*.

8 At a tarmac lane below Tor y Foel, keep **straight ahead**, crossing the lane and climbing a steep grassy slope. Pass a small cairn marking the summit and continue along an obvious path to the east. Drop through a narrow section of common to a metal gate at the bottom. Cross a stile and descend along a sunken bridleway to a lane.

***SC**: To bypass Tor y Foel, **turn right** on the lane below the mountain and follow it to its end. Keep **straight ahead** past a farm onto a track along the side of the hill. The bridleway, marked *Beacons Way*, bears right after about 700m and descends to a lane. **Turn left** for about 300m as far as Pen-y-bailey, where the main route is rejoined at point **9**.

9 Cross the lane onto a farm access road. **Bear left** in the farmyard and cross a grassy area to a *Beacons Way* marker on a metal gate. Go through the gate and **turn right** towards the next metal gate. Follow the left edge of a field down to a stile above a large farmhouse and cross an access road to the gate **on the left**.

10 Follow the right edge of a field to a stile. Drop down the next field to a stile on the left and head across the middle of a field past a telegraph pole. Cross a stile into a lightly wooded area and **bear right**. Descend to a footbridge over the Monmouthshire & Brecon Canal and **turn right** along the towpath.

11 Follow the towpath as far as Bridge *130* (for the Coach & Horses, leave the towpath at Bridge *133*). Cross the bridge and follow a waymarked path through three fields, keeping a small stream to your left. In the **fourth** field, **turn left** through a gateway, then **right**, up a long, narrow field with the stream to your right. Cross a road and **turn left** along the pavement. A gravel path **on the right** leads back to the car park.

THE 'BWLCH' OR 'GAP ROAD' FROM FAN Y BIG. PHOTO: TRACY BURTON

11 The Llanfrynach Horseshoe

16.5km/10.2miles

A circuit of Cwm Oergwm from Llanfrynach along two fine ridges and a dramatic escarpment.

Llanfrynach » Bwlch y Ddwyallt (754m) » Fan y Bîg (719m) » Llanfrynach

Start

On-street parking by the public toilets opposite the church in Llanfrynach. GR: SO 074257.

The Walk

This straightforward circuit tackles two of the Brecon Beacons' more easterly peaks, Bwlch y Ddwyallt and Fan y Bîg. Two fine ridges either side of Cwm Oergwm provide access to and from the summits, which are linked by a dramatic escarpment walk above the head of the valley. Views of the higher summits to the west are simply superb.

We begin from the centre of Llanfrynach, a pretty village southeast of Brecon. Lanes and tracks climb to the edge of the common and a long but steady ascent, which skirts the western slopes of Bryn, to a junction of paths at Rhiw Bwlch y Ddwyallt. From here a diversion is possible to a memorial cairn below Cwar y Gigfran, where a Wellington bomber crashed into the mountain in July 1942, killing all five Canadian crew members. Debris from the plane still litters the slopes.

Turning west, we follow the curving escarpment over Bwlch y Ddwyallt and along Craig Cwareli. The view across Cwm Oergwm is spectacular, with the peaks of Fan y Bîg, Cribyn, Pen y Fan and Corn Du all lined up, one behind the other (photo p75). After passing around the head of Cwm Oergwm, we fork right to follow the gentle slope up to Fan y Bîg, where a projecting slab of stone known as 'the diving board' provides a great photo opportunity. Far below is 'the gap road', an ancient trackway through the mountains linking Brecon and Merthyr (see walk 12).

Pleasant walking along Cwm Cyff leads to an easy descent off the common. A rough track takes us down to a lane at Pen-yr-heol, which we leave to cross fields towards Nant Menasgin. This delightful little river takes us back to Llanfrynach, with the possibility of a drink in the White Swan.

THE LLANFRYNACH HORSESHOE

DISTANCE: 16.5KM/10.2MILES » **TOTAL ASCENT:** 687M/2,254FT » **START GR:** SO 074257 » **TIME:** ALLOW 6 HOURS **MAP:** OS EXPLORER OL12, BRECON BEACONS NATIONAL PARK WESTERN AREA, 1:25,000 » **REFRESHMENTS:** THE WHITE SWAN, LLANFRYNACH » **NAVIGATION:** FAIRLY EASY IN GOOD WEATHER, BUT MAY PRESENT DIFFICULTY IN POOR VISIBILITY.

Fan y Big
5
4
22
Cwm Cynwyn
Cefn Cyff
LLANFRYNACH
Cwm Oergwm
Cwm Cwareli
Craig Cwmoergwm
Craig Cwareli
Bwlch y Ddwyallt
Rhiw Bwlch y Ddwyallt
Gwaun Cerrig Llwydion
Graig Fan Las
Memorial
Waun Rydd
Cwar y Gigfran
Craig Pwllfa
Carn Pica
Craig y Fan
Cefn Bach
Cefn Edmwnt
Gist Wen
Ffordd Las or Bwlch Main
Enclosure
House Platform
Nant y Llanerch
Nantllannerch
Twyn Du
Pant-y-gelynen
Cwm Banw
Blaen Cwm Banw
Fords
Ford
Waterfall
Waterfalls
Cefn y Bryn
Bryn
Cairn

11 THE LLANFRYNACH HORSESHOE

Directions – The Llanfrynach Horseshoe

S Facing the public toilets, **turn left** along the pavement. Almost immediately, **turn right** along a narrow village street and continue to a T-junction. **Turn right**, crossing Nant Menasgin. About 100m past the bridge, **turn right** onto Tregaer Road.

2 Climb along a lane for about 700m. Look out for a gate on the left across a farm lane. This is marked as a footpath and signed to *Rhiw Bwlch y Ddwyallt*. **Turn left** through the gate and follow a tarmac lane across a stream and up a hill on the far side. Where the tarmac ends (there are farm ruins to the left), **turn right** through a gate onto a gravel track. Go through a second gate a short distance ahead and immediately **turn left**. You are now heading uphill, away from the track, alongside a fence.

3 At the next gate/stile, **bear slightly right**, heading straight up the hill. Climb to a flatter area with woodland and a boundary wall/fence to your right. From here, the correct way ahead can appear confusing, with a number of competing paths criss-crossing the hillside. **Aim to the right of Bryn** – the high ground immediately ahead of you – and join a path climbing diagonally across the slope to the west of its summit. Emerge on the crest of the ridge and continue upwards to a junction of paths at Rhiw Bwlch y Ddwyallt.

> OR To visit the memorial cairn (see walk introduction), **bear left** and follow a contouring path south-east for about 700m. The memorial is located just below the escarpment crest at grid reference SO 061200. Return the same way.

4 **Turn right** and follow a curving escarpment over Bwlch y Ddwyallt. Pass around the head of Cwm Oergwm and **fork right** towards Fan y Bîg. Keep **straight ahead** to the summit's northwest end and the projecting slab of stone known as 'the diving board'.

5 Descend along the 'snout' of Fan y Bîg, following the crest of Cefn Cyff roughly northeast. A grassy path off the end of the ridge leads down to a bridlegate in the far corner of the common. Continue onto a rough, stony track and descend to a lane by Pen-yr-heol Barn. **Turn left** down the lane, signed *Llanfrynach*.

6 About 300m down the road, **turn right** at a footpath sign through a wooden gate. Head straight across a field towards a gate on the far side, then follow the right edge of the next field down to a lane. Cross to a bridlegate and continue along the left edge of a field.

7 Go through a new gate near Tynllwyn and along the left edge of a field. In the next field, **bear left** to a waymark post, then follow the arrow right along a line of trees and down to a river (Nant Menasgin). **Turn left** and follow the river down to a lane near Tyfry Farm. **Turn right**, passing the farm, and enter Llanfrynach. **Turn right** at a T-junction to return to your starting point. The White Swan Inn is just around the left-hand bend ahead.

LEFT TO RIGHT: CORN DU, PEN Y FAN, CRIBYN, FAN Y BIG PHOTO: TRACY BURTON

CRIBYN FROM PEN Y FAN. PHOTO: ADAM LONG

12 The Taf Fechan Skyline

13.1km/8.1miles

The classic traverse of the Beacons escarpment.

Taf Fechan Forest » Bwlch ar y Fan » Cribyn (795m) » Pen y Fan (886m) » Corn Du (873m) » Lower Neuadd Reservoir » Taf Fechan Forest

Start

Neuadd Forestry Commission car park off the minor road between Talybont-on-Usk and Pontsticill.
GR: SO 037169.

The Walk

This is one of the most popular circuits in the National Park, so best left for a quieter day. The route takes in the two highest peaks in the park (Pen y Fan and Corn Du), along with the third highest peak in the Brecon Beacons proper (Cribyn) – not to mention a fine escarpment above the Taf Fechan valley. The scenery is superb, but the climbs up Cribyn and Pen y Fan can feel relentless. Fortunately, the first of these can be bypassed easily, reducing the amount of height gain without detracting from the overall quality of the walk.

Our walk begins with a steady climb along an ancient trackway known locally as 'the gap road'. This ascends across the eastern side of the Taf Fechan valley to Bwlch ar y Fan (the 'gap'), a deep col between Fan y Bîg and Cribyn. As we climb, there are good views across the Upper Neuadd Reservoir towards the valley's western escarpment, along which we will be returning later.

At Bwlch ar y Fan we have a choice. The main route climbs steeply to the top of Cribyn, but there is also an obvious path which skirts the base of the mountain to the left. Both routes rejoin for the steep climb up Pen y Fan, which cannot be avoided. On a fine weekend, the summit is likely to be packed with visitors who have followed the direct route up from the Storey Arms.

Beyond Corn Du, we turn south along the escarpment edge above Gwaun Taf. A tricky descent over loose scree leads down to the Lower Neuadd Reservoir, a delightful spot surrounded in season by a colourful profusion of rhododendrons. A short stroll down the reservoir access road takes us back to our starting point.

THE TAF FECHAN SKYLINE

DISTANCE: 13.1KM/8.1MILES » **TOTAL ASCENT:** 658M/2,159FT » **START GR:** SO 037169 » **TIME:** ALLOW 5 HOURS **MAP:** OS EXPLORER OL12, BRECON BEACONS NATIONAL PARK WESTERN AREA, 1:25,000 » **REFRESHMENTS:** NONE ON ROUTE; NEARBY ARE THE OLD BARN TEA ROOM, YSTRADGYNWYN, AND THE RED COW, PONTSTICILL » **NAVIGATION:** CLEAR PATHS ALL THE WAY, BUT NOT RECOMMENDED IN POOR VISIBILITY.

WALKERS BELOW CORN DU PHOTO: ADAM LONG

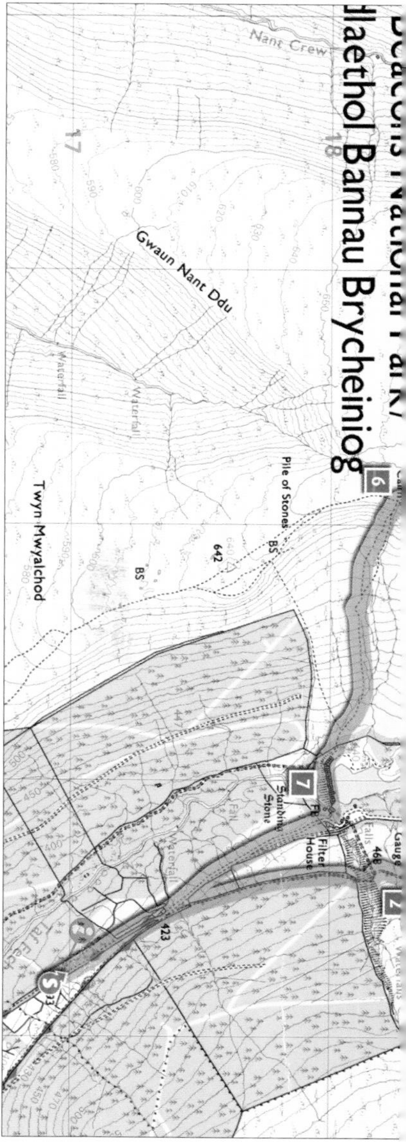

12 THE TAF FECHAN SKYLINE

Directions – The Taf Fechan Skyline

S Walk to the far end of the car park and follow a gravel path up to the reservoir access road. **Turn left**, soon reaching a junction of two tracks with the tarmac road. **Fork right** onto the second of these, a rough track which climbs steadily along the edge of forestry to a gate.

2 Once through the gate, drop steeply to cross a stream in a gully. As you emerge from the gully, **fork right** on the more obvious track, which follows a steady ascent across the slopes above Upper Neuadd Reservoir to the deep col between Fan y Bîg and Cribyn.

3 At the top of the pass, climb the steep slope **on the left** to the summit of Cribyn. From the top, **turn left** and descend steeply into a col. A steep, stone-pitched path climbs to the summit of Pen y Fan.

SC ***SC**: To bypass Cribyn, follow the obvious path skirting **round the left** of Cribyn and rejoin the main route on the climb up Pen y Fan.

4 On Pen y Fan, **bear slightly left** from the summit cairn and descend on a wide path into the col below Corn Du.

SC ***SC**: To bypass Corn Du, follow the wide path **to the left** of the mountain. Rejoin the main route at the junction of paths in Bwlch Duwynt.

Fork right up the short, easy ascent to the top. **Turn left** at the summit and descend to a junction of paths in Bwlch Duwynt.

5 **Fork left** off the wide path and follow the escarpment edge south. Cross the narrow ridge between Cwm Crew and Gwaun Taf and continue along high cliffs above the Neuadd reservoirs.

6 **Turn left** at a large cairn onto a steep, tricky descent over loose scree. This soon turns into a pleasant grassy path descending towards the Lower Neuadd Reservoir. Go through a metal gate at the bottom of the common and follow a grassy path along the top of the dam.

7 Cross the overflow channel and pass to the left of a derelict stone tower. Climb to an access road by a stone building and **turn right**. Rejoin your outward route by the junction of tracks. Keep an eye out for the gravel path back to the car park, about 150m past the junction.

PEN Y FAN SUMMIT PHOTO: TRACY BURTON

LOOKING DOWN CEFN CWM LLWCH FROM PEN Y FAN PHOTO: ADAM LONG

13 Pen y Fan & the Cwm Llwch Horseshoe

11km/6.8miles

The connoisseur's approach to the highest peak in South Wales.

Cwm Gwdi » Pen y Fan (886m) » Corn Du (873m) » Llyn Cwm Llwch » Cwm Llwch » Cwm Gwdi

Start

National Trust car park at the end of a narrow lane south of Brecon.
GR: SO 025249.

The Walk

Pen y Fan is without doubt the most popular peak in the national park, attracting hordes of walkers each fine weekend up the short ascent from the Storey Arms. By starting from the end of a narrow lane south of Brecon, this route avoids the worst of the crowds, and also includes what is undoubtedly the most dramatic approach to the summit, from beneath the mountain's towering northeast face.

We begin from the National Trust car park in Cwm Gwdi. A track leads onto the mountain and climbs steeply to the top of Cefn Cwm Llwch, a long ridge extending north from Pen y Fan. A section of level walking allows us to appreciate the full majesty of the mountain ahead before the final steep clamber onto its wide, tabletop summit. After the long climb from Cwm Gwdi, the sheer number of people congregated here on a fine day can be quite a shock.

Leaving the summit, we head west along the escarpment to the subsidiary top of Corn Du. A steep path to the north-west, ledged in places, continues along the high cliffs of Craig Cwm Llwch past an obelisk where the body of Tommy Jones was discovered in September 1900. Five-year-old Tommy had got lost almost a month before near his grandparents' farmhouse in Cwm Llwch, and how he managed to find his way onto such an exposed ridge remains a mystery.

Just past the obelisk, we fork right, descending steeply to the glacial lake of Llyn Cwm Llwch. A delightful grassy track continues down the valley, dropping easily across lightly wooded slopes to a vehicle track by a house. The track turns to tarmac below a picnic area, and we then follow quiet lanes for a little over two kilometres back to our starting point.

PEN Y FAN & THE CWM LLWCH HORSESHOE

DISTANCE: 11.0KM/6.8MILES » **TOTAL ASCENT:** 643M/2,110FT » **START GR:** SO 025249 » **TIME:** ALLOW 4.5 HOURS **MAP:** OS EXPLORER OL12, BRECON BEACONS NATIONAL PARK WESTERN AREA, 1:25,000 » **REFRESHMENTS:** NONE ON ROUTE; NEARBY IS THE TAI'R BULL INN, LIBANUS, AS WELL AS PLENTY OF CHOICE IN BRECON » **NAVIGATION:** EASY IN FINE WEATHER BUT NOT RECOMMENDED IN POOR VISIBILITY.

Directions – Pen y Fan & the Cwm Llwch Horseshoe

S Walk up to the end of the lane and go through a gate onto a track. This curves round the **right edge** of a rough field to a gate onto open common. Follow the wide but faint grassy track up the hill ahead.

2 As the track steepens, it bears slightly left, becoming stonier and more defined. Once onto Cefn Cwm Llwch, the gradient eases and Pen y Fan's towering north-east face becomes visible ahead.

3 As the summit draws nearer, the gradient steepens considerably. Clamber up steep rocky steps to emerge onto a wide, flat – and often very crowded – summit area.

4 **Bear right**, picking up a wide gravel path running west along the escarpment edge, and drop into a shallow saddle between Pen y Fan and the neighbouring summit of Corn Du. **Fork right** and climb easily up to the latter.

5 From Corn Du, take a steep path descending northwest along the high cliffs of Craig Cwm Llwch. **Continue along** the escarpment past the Tommy Jones obelisk, then **fork right** onto a path down to Llyn Cwm Llwch.

6 From the lake, follow the obvious grassy track down the valley. This descends easily along Cwm Llwch, eventually leaving the open common and dropping through fields to a gate in front of a cottage. **Turn left** over a stile to bypass the house. At the end of the wall, **bear right** to rejoin the main track below the house.

7 Continue along a broad vehicle track to a grassy parking area. Keep **straight ahead** onto a lane and follow it down to a T-junction. **Turn right** for about 1.5km. On a sharp left-hand bend, **turn right** and cross a cattle grid by a National Trust sign for *Cwm Gwdi*. Follow the lane back up the hill to your starting point.

13 PEN Y FAN & THE CWM LLWCH HORSESHOE

SECTION 3

Fforest Fawr

The eastern edge of Fforest Fawr is marked by the deep line of the Taf and Tarell valleys; another valley pairing, the Crai and Tawe, provides its boundary to the west. Although the peaks of Fforest Fawr lack the majesty and distinction found in other regions of the National Park, the area's extensive upland will appeal to those who enjoy the solitude of wild, open moorland. South of the hills, deep wooded valleys and spectacular waterfalls form a distinctive sub-region, 'waterfall country'. Walking here is an unforgettable experience, but the area can get very busy on weekends and bank holidays.

SGWD GWLADUS PHOTO: TRACY BURTON

THE VIEW DOWN CWM TAF FROM FAN FAWR PHOTO: TRACY BURTON

CRAIG CERRIG-GLEISIAD PHOTO: ADAM LONG

14 Craig Cerrig-gleisiad & Fan Fawr 12.1km/7.5miles

A unique glacial cirque and Fforest Fawr's highest peak.

Craig Cerrig-gleisiad National Nature Reserve » Twyn Dylluan-ddu » Fan Frynych (629m) » Craig Cerrig-gleisiad (629m) » Fan Fawr (734m) » Storey Arms » Craig Cerrig-gleisiad National Nature Reserve

Start

Lay-by on the west side of the A470 about 3km north of the Storey Arms. GR: SN 971222.

The Walk

The starting point for this walk is the impressive natural amphitheatre of Craig Cerrig-gleisiad: a glacial cirque framed by dramatic, ice-carved crags and littered with moraine and other Ice Age debris. A precipitous north-facing headwall still creates a microclimate cold enough to make Craig Cerrig-gleisiad the southernmost location in Britain for a number of rare arctic-alpine plants. Along with nearby Fan Frynych, the area is a designated National Nature Reserve.

Our walk begins with a short climb up to the lip of Craig Cerrig-gleisiad's bowl-shaped hollow. Avoiding a direct assault on the valley's plunging headwall, we climb obliquely across the hill towards a finger of high ground extending north to Twyn Dylluan-ddu. Turning back on ourselves, we follow a track up the spur to the summit of Fan Frynych and then continue along the high cliffs that form the valley headwall.

Leaving the cliffs, we strike out across open moor towards Fan Fawr, a bulky hill about three kilometres to the south. Views to the east are dominated by the majestic peaks of Corn Du and Pen y Fan, though our own route is refreshingly free from the crowds that so often blight these mountains.

A narrow, contouring path takes us around Fan Fawr's north-east flank to join a well-worn path from the Storey Arms. After a steep climb to the top, we retrace our steps and descend to the former coaching inn (now an outdoor centre). A fine stone track that was once the main coach road takes us down the Tarell valley, leaving one final climb across a steeply sloping field to finish.

CRAIG CERRIG-GLEISIAD & FAN FAWR

DISTANCE: 12.1KM/7.5MILES » **TOTAL ASCENT:** 667M/2,188FT » **START GR:** SN 971222 » **TIME:** ALLOW 5 HOURS **MAP:** OS EXPLORER OL12, BRECON BEACONS NATIONAL PARK WESTERN AREA, 1:25,000 » **REFRESHMENTS:** NONE ON ROUTE; NEARBY IS THE TAI'R BULL INN, LIBANUS, AND TEA ROOMS AT THE NATIONAL PARK VISITOR CENTRE ON MYNYDD ILLTUD COMMON » **NAVIGATION:** STRAIGHTFORWARD IN FINE WEATHER, BUT THE MOORLAND CROSSING TO FAN FAWR IS DIFFICULT IN POOR VISIBILITY.

PEN Y FAN FROM FAN FAWR PHOTO: TRACY BURTON

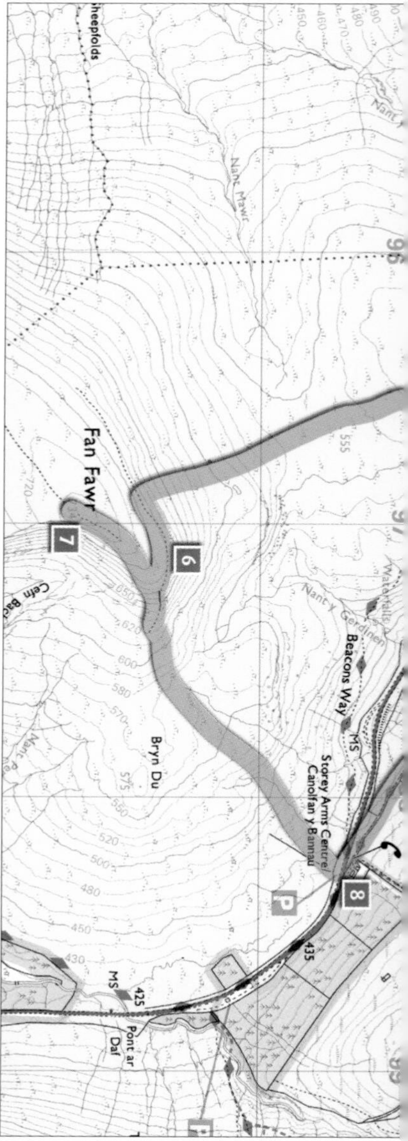

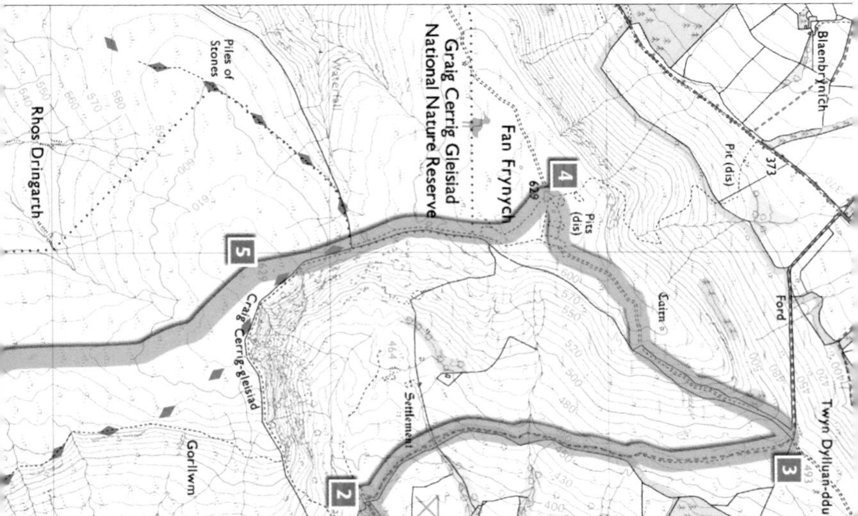

14 CRAIG CERRIG-GLEISIAD & FAN FAWR

Directions – Craig Cerrig-gleisiad & Fan Fawr

S From the lay-by, go through a kissing gate onto a gravel path signed *Twyn Dylluan-ddu & Forest Lodge*. Pass an information board and climb through trees to a wooden gate in a dry-stone wall. Straight ahead are the towering crags of Craig Cerrig-gleisiad.

2 Go through a gap in the wall and immediately **turn right**. Follow a grassy path along-side the wall, climbing obliquely up the slope of the hill. Stay with the wall, crossing two narrow gullies carved by streams. Where the wall falls away down the slope, keep **straight ahead** across the open hill. Climb gradually but steadily to a kissing gate leading onto the outside bend of a gravel track.

3 **Turn left** onto the track and climb steeply to a metal gate and stile. Continue climbing across rough terrain until the track levels out on a spur of high ground extending north-east from Fan Frynych. Where a wider plateau is reached, **bear right** onto a grassy path towards the summit trig point of Fan Frynych (the path begins on a left-hand bend at the top of a short rise; the trig point is not immediately visible).

4 From the summit, **bear left** onto a wider grassy path to return to the track, which continues along the top of Craig Cerrig-gleisiad's high cliffs. **Do not** cross the fence on your left, but drop to a stile and gate in a shallow valley by a pond. Cross the stile and **continue straight** up the hill ahead. A pile of stones marks the summit of Craig Cerrig-gleisiad.

5 **Bear slightly left** from the stones, onto a faint path crossing the wide, open moor towards Fan Fawr. As you approach the mountain's steep northern slopes, **fork right** towards a small crag. Pass to the right of this and climb steeply to a narrow ledge path contouring across the slope. **Turn left** and follow the path around the mountain's north-eastern flank.

6 Maintaining height, continue around the mountain until an obvious grassy path is met (this is the main track ascending from the Storey Arms). **Turn right** and climb steeply to a cairn marking the summit of Fan Fawr. It is possible to continue to a trig point about 600m south-west of the summit.

7 Either way, return down the steep slope climbed earlier and continue downhill in the direction of the Storey Arms. Keep **straight ahead** across a flatter marshy area, aiming for the obvious gravel path that can be seen climbing the hill on the far side of the valley. Once over a small rise, drop to a car park on the A470 opposite the Storey Arms.

8 Cross the busy main road towards a red telephone box. **Turn left** onto a track signed *Taff Trail*, which takes a parallel line to the A470 on an old coaching road along Glyn Tarell. Descend steadily, passing a National Trust sign at a gate for *Blaenglyn Farm* and crossing a stone bridge over a stream. Just before a second bridge, **turn left** over a stile onto a path signed to *Llwyn-y-celyn Youth Hostel*. **Bear left** across a field to a stile and follow a short section of track down to a wooden bridge across Afon Tarell.

9 **Ignore** the signed path right to the youth hostel and keep **straight ahead** up a steep field towards two trees on the brow of the hill. Continue past the trees to a stile at the top of the field and **turn right** onto the A470. Cross the road carefully to return to your starting point on the west side of the road.

CATTLE GRAZING ABOVE CRAIG CERRIG-GLEISIAD; PEN Y FAN AND CORN DU BEYOND PHOTO: TRACY BURTON

THE NEDD FECHAN NEAR THE SARN HELEN CROSSING. PHOTO: TRACY BURTON

15 Fan Nedd & Fan Gyhirych

19.6km/12.2miles

Peace and solitude in the heart of Fforest Fawr.

Blaen Llia » Fan Nedd (663m) » Bwlch y Duwynt » Fan Gyhirych (725m) » Sarn Helen » Blaen Llia

Start

Blaen Llia Forestry Commission car park, just off the minor road between Sennybridge and Ystradfellte. GR: SN 927164.

The Walk

Perhaps because it lacks spectacular peaks, Fforest Fawr is one of the least frequented parts of the national park, and consequently one that recommends itself to those who like the peace and solitude of wide, open spaces. The present walk takes in two of the area's principal summits (the first optional) and is a good introduction to the region as a whole.

We begin from the Forestry Commission car park at Blaen Llia. Almost immediately, we are faced with the choice of a steep and potentially boggy ascent up Fan Nedd or of a road walk to the head of the valley, where the mountain can be bypassed via a contouring path across its northern face. Tough or easy: the choice is ours!

The ascent of the second peak, Fan Gyhirych, is much less strenuous and follows a wide vehicle track for part of the way. The wide summit plateau is not that inspiring initially, but its north and west edges, where the land falls sharply away, provide some of the best vantage points in Fforest Fawr.

Gentler southern slopes take us back down to the track and on into a wild, remote valley pocked with old quarries. A legacy of stone vehicle tracks keeps feet dry across the rough, boggy moorland. Eventually, we reach the former Roman road of Sarn Helen – a stony track connecting the fortresses of Nidum (Neath) and Cicucium (Y Gaer near Brecon) – and drop to cross the Nedd Fechan at a delightful spot.

A steep climb follows to a large standing stone marking a Roman grave. Intriguingly, the stone is known as Maen Madoc ('Madoc's stone'), though it is inscribed in Latin to an unknown Roman called Dervacus. A gentle downhill stroll through forest takes us back to our starting point.

FAN NEDD & FAN GYHIRYCH

DISTANCE: 19.6KM/12.2MILES » **TOTAL ASCENT:** 684M/2,244FT » **START GR:** SN 927164 » **TIME:** ALLOW 6.5 HOURS **MAP:** OS EXPLORER OL12, BRECON BEACONS NATIONAL PARK WESTERN AREA, 1:25,000 » **REFRESHMENTS:** NONE ON ROUTE; NEAREST OPTION IS THE NEW INN, YSTRADFELLTE » **NAVIGATION:** MAINLY ON GOOD, CLEAR TRACKS.

MAEN MADOC PHOTO: TRACY BURTON

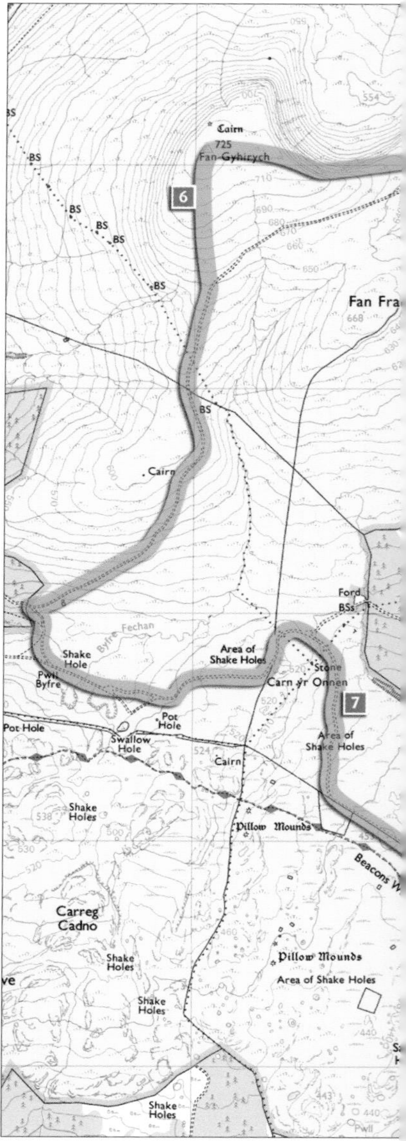

15 FAN NEDD & FAN GYHIRYCH

Directions – Fan Nedd & Fan Gyhirych

S From the car park, walk back up the access track to the road and **turn right**. Cross a cattle grid and **turn left** over a stile marked with an open access symbol.

> OR To avoid a steep and potentially boggy climb up Fan Nedd, **continue north** along the road for about 3km. At the head of the valley, just before the road plunges steeply down the far side, **turn left** over a stile and follow a path climbing along the left edge of a wall. After levelling off, contour across the steep north face of Fan Nedd, high above the upper Senni valley. Rejoin the main route at point **4** in a col (Bwlch y Duwynt) between the headwaters of the Senni and Nedd Fechan rivers.

2 Keep **straight ahead** up the slope, picking up a clear path parallel to the edge of the forestry plantation on the left. Cross a small stream and **bear right**, along the line of the stream, towards the high ground of Fan Nedd. Marshy ground means the path is not always clear, but keep aiming for the highest and steepest part of the mountain. Once over the brow, a clear path leads along a ridge to the summit trig point.

3 From the trig point, keep **straight ahead** along the ridge to a well-built cairn at the northern end of the summit area. After admiring the views, **bear left** onto a path descending north-west to a pass between the Senni and Nedd Fechan valleys (Bwlch y Duwynt).

4 Cross a marshy area to a gap in a stone wall and a rough track ascending to the right. Follow the track up to the next gateway, but **do not** go through it. Instead, **turn left** and follow the line of the fence up a rough field (there is no defined path). At the top of the field, cross a stile by sheep pens onto a gravel vehicle track.

5 **Turn left** along the track and climb easily up the eastern slopes of Fan Gyhirych. On a left-hand bend, keep **straight ahead** onto a grassy path and climb more steeply; Cray Reservoir is soon visible to the right. Once up, cross a plateau to the summit trig point. For even better views, walk 100m north to a cairn on the plateau edge.

6 Leave the mountain via the gentler slopes to the south and rejoin the track left earlier. Descend to a gate and continue downwards into a wild valley scarred by the remains of quarry workings. With a forestry plantation ahead, **turn left** onto a track curving left round the valley in front of two former quarries. When a second forestry plantation appears ahead, **fork right** onto a rough grassy track and over a metal gate.

7 Follow the track down to a dilapidated dry-stone wall and **bear left**, alongside the wall. The track narrows to a path. Eventually, **bear left**, away from the wall, to a junction with a good-quality track.

8 **Turn right** onto the track, which descends gently across moorland parallel to the Nedd Fechan valley on the left. Where the Beacons Way joins from the right, keep **straight ahead**, following a sign for *Sarn Helen*.

9 At a junction of tracks by the corner of a forestry plantation, **turn left** through a metal farm gate (the track is signed *Sarn Helen* in both directions). Follow the track as it curves left and drops to the Nedd Fechan river. Cross by a footbridge and continue up the track ahead.

10 Climb steeply until the track levels off near the Roman grave of Maen Madoc. Continue through a forestry plantation, descending gently to a junction with a lane. **Turn right** for about 400m, then **drop left** on the access track to the Blaen Llia car park.

BEHIND SGWD YR EIRA PHOTO: TRACY BURTON

16 The Waterfalls Roundabout

15km/9.3miles

An exhilarating circuit around South Wales' most spectacular waterfalls.

Cwm Porth » Sgŵd Clun-gwyn » Sgwd yr Eira » Craig y Ddinas » Pontneddfechan » Sgwd Gwladus – Scŵd Ddwli » Pont Melin-fach » Pont Rhyd-y-cnau » Gwaun Bryn-bwch » Cwm Porth

Start

Pay and display car park at Cwm Porth about 1km south of Ystradfellte.
GR: SN 928124.

The Walk

Water is the dominant theme of this walk, which links the region's most spectacular waterfalls in one exhilarating circuit. Although all the falls are worth seeing, the highlight is undoubtedly walking behind Sgwd yr Eira, a wall of water negotiated by a rocky ledge between the fall and the cliff face. Take your time and follow any warning signs posted.

We begin from Cwm Porth, close to where the River Mellte disappears underground for some 250m. Following the resurgent river downstream, we pass through pleasant meadows and woodland to a viewpoint overlooking our first significant fall, Sgŵd Clun-gwyn. Walkers are discouraged from using the unprotected path below this point, so we follow a good-quality path along the rim of the gorge, higher up. Two further falls can be visited along a signed link path.

We now approach the walk's most thrilling moment: the roaring wall of Sgwd yr Eira. A steep climb takes us out of the gorge and on to a well-signed path to Craig y Ddinas. On the way, there are further opportunities for detours to waterfalls on the smaller Sychryd river.

About halfway round, Pontneddfechan is ideally situated for a refreshment stop. Leaving the village, we follow a good-quality track along the Nedd Fechan to Pont Melin-fach. This is a delightful section, offering good views of a number of smaller falls. A short distance up the Pyrddin is Sgwd Gwladus, possibly the prettiest waterfall on the walk.

Between Pont Melin-fach and Pont Rhyd-y-cnau the path is narrow, undulating and rugged, and may take longer than expected. Leaving the river, we climb on a steep track to the fine views of Gwaun Bryn-bwch. A bridleway – which may be muddy in places – leads gently back to the car park.

THE WATERFALLS ROUNDABOUT

DISTANCE: 15KM/9.3MILES » **TOTAL ASCENT:** 412M/1,352FT » **START GR:** SN 928124 » **TIME:** ALLOW 5 HOURS
MAP: OS EXPLORER OL12, BRECON BEACONS NATIONAL PARK WESTERN AREA, 1:25,000 » **REFRESHMENTS:** OLD WHITE HORSE INN AND ANGEL INN, PONTNEDDFECHAN; A SHORT DRIVE FROM WALK START/FINISH IS THE NEW INN, YSTRADFELLTE
NAVIGATION: WELL-SIGNED PATHS THROUGHOUT.

THE AFON MELLTE *PHOTO: TRACY BURTON*

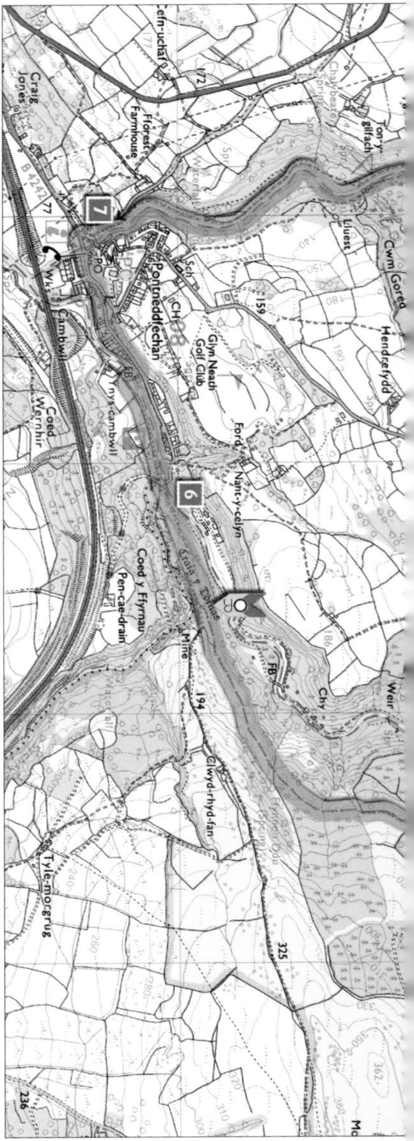

16 THE WATERFALLS ROUNDABOUT

Directions – The Waterfalls Roundabout

S A signed path descends from the car park to the cave entrance at Porth yr Ogof. After viewing the cave, return to the car park entrance and cross the road to a path signed *Sgwd Clun-gwyn* and *Blue Pool.* After passing an *Access for Cavers* sign, the path swings right, down a rough, rocky section, to continue through meadows alongside Afon Mellte. Follow the obvious path along the river as far as a footbridge on the right.

2 **Do not** cross the bridge, but **continue ahead**, following a sign for *Sgwd Clun-gwyn.* Where the path forks, **bear left**, away from the river, and climb to a higher level path with a wooden fence on the right. At a waymarked junction, **turn right** onto a cobbled path, zigzagging down between wooden fences to a viewpoint overlooking Sgŵd Clun-gwyn. Return to the junction at the top of the path and **turn right**, signed *Sgwd yr Eira.*

> OR From the viewpoint above Sgŵd Clun-gwyn it is possible to follow a lower, unprotected path along the river to the next fall, Sgŵd Isaf Clun-gwyn. A signed path from here continues past Sgŵd y Pannwr and back to the main route above the gorge. However, the path below Sgŵd Clun-gwyn is narrow and exposed and not recommended for inexperienced walkers. The two falls can be visited more safely via a signed detour from the main route (see below).

3 A good quality path, part of the Four Falls Trail, winds high above the gorge and the river below. Continue past a signed path for *Sgŵd y Pannwr* on the right and follow the main path as it curves left above the Hepste gorge. At the second of two closely spaced benches, **turn right** down a steep, stepped path signed to *Sgwd yr Eira.*

> OR Sgŵd y Pannwr and Sgŵd Isaf Clun-gwyn can be visited by following the signed path on the right. This is the path ascended if following the optional route from Sgŵd Clun-gwyn.

4 Drop to the riverbed and clamber across boulders towards the wall of water ahead. Cross the wet stone ledge behind the fall and start climbing out of the gorge on a rough, stony path that soon turns to gravel. The path climbs to a junction by an information board for the Sgwd yr Eira Trail. **Turn right**, signed *Craig y Ddinas.*

5 Pass through a mixture of woodland and open moorland, enjoying fine views across the Mellte valley. Continue to follow signs for *Craig y Ddinas* and join a gravel track

along the ridge between the Mellte and Sychryd rivers. Descend steeply to the car park at Craig y Ddinas.

OR To visit another fine fall and an old silica mine, **turn sharp left** at the gravel track, shortly curving right and descending to the Sychryd river. A further cascade of falls can be seen by following a wide, level track for about 400m up the Sychryd from Craig y Ddinas car park.

6 **Turn left** at the entrance to the car park, then **right**, down a track signed as a bridleway. About 100m before a house, **turn right** through a gate and cross a narrow strip of pasture to a footbridge over the Mellte river. **Turn left** along the road, keeping straight ahead at a T-junction by the Dinas Inn.

7 Just past the Angel Inn is the Waterfalls Centre. To continue with the walk, **join a gravel track behind the pub** – part of The Elidir Trail – signed to *Pont Melin-fach* and *Sgwd Gwladus*. A wide, good quality track follows the Nedd Fechan upstream to where the Pyrddin joins from the left. Cross to the far bank of the Pyrddin and **turn left**, following a path upstream signed to *Sgwd Gwladus*.

8 After viewing the fall, return to the confluence of the Pyrddin and Nedd Fechan and **turn left** (signed *Pont Melin-fach*). The path continues alongside the Nedd Fechan, passing a number of waterfalls. A picnic area and car park is reached at Pont Melin-fach.

9 Cross the river by a road bridge and **turn left** onto a path signed to *Pont Rhyd-y-cnau*. If river levels allow, take the lower path directly ahead, passing below a wet, dripping bank then **swinging right** to rejoin the easier, upper path. The narrow, undulating path continues through a wild wooded gorge as far as Pont Rhyd-y-cnau, where a rough track bridges the river. **Turn right** up the track, which is signed to *Gwaun Bryn-bwch*.

10 Climb steeply through woodland, then across more open ground, to a gate onto a lane. **Turn right** along the lane, shortly reaching a wider road at a T-junction. **Turn left** for a few metres, then **turn right** onto a track signed to *Porth yr Ogof*. Follow the track gently downhill until a blue bridleway arrow directs you to **fork left** onto an enclosed path. The path passes through a number of gates, eventually emerging on the road opposite the entrance to Cwm Porth car park.

SECTION 4

The Black Mountain

The Black Mountain is the wildest, most remote region of the National Park, including areas of upland more than 5km away from the nearest public highway. The long bridleways crossing this large tract of moorland are indistinct and difficult to follow, and most walkers tend to stick to the Beacons Way and the well-worn routes to Llyn y Fan Fach and Fan Brycheiniog (802m). Outside the main massif, there are some fine, gentler hills and numerous pretty river valleys.

NANT TAWE FECHAN *PHOTO: TRACY BURTON*

LLYN Y FAN FACH AND BANNAU SIR GAER. PHOTO: TRACY BURTON

CRAIG-Y-NOS COUNTRY PARK PHOTO: TRACY BURTON

17 Cribarth & Henrhyd Falls

13.2km/8.2miles

A 'sleeping giant' and the highest waterfall in South Wales.

Craig-y-nos Country Park » Cribarth (423m) » Ynyswen » Henrhyd Falls » Pen-y-cae » Craig-y-nos Country Park

Start

Pay-and-display car park at Craig-y-nos Country Park. GR: SN 839155.

The Walk

Craig-y-nos Country Park provides the starting point for this superbly varied circuit, which includes mountain, moorland, a wooded ravine, and the highest waterfall in South Wales. The park itself is set in an idyllic spot on the banks of the River Tawe and is worth exploring thoroughly.

We begin by heading south along the A4067 past Craig-y-nos Castle. Now a hotel, this Victorian Gothic building was home between 1878 and 1919 to world-renowned opera singer Adelina Patti. The country park at that time was part of the castle's private estate.

Our first objective is the summit of Cribarth, known locally as 'the sleeping giant' because of its profile when viewed from the south. We ascend via a concessionary path from Craig-y-nos Quarry, climbing steeply but quickly onto the open hill. Impressive limestone crags surround the summit and the remains of extensive quarrying activity can also be seen. The summit provides excellent all-round views and is a good place to appreciate the full extent of the Black Mountain: the vast, empty wilderness rising above Cribarth to the north.

After a pleasant descent to Ynyswen, we pick up an undulating path along the side of a deep, thickly wooded ravine. Following the small river of Nant Llech upstream, we walk the full length of this atmospheric gorge, eventually reaching a natural amphitheatre into which the water from Henrhyd Falls plunges unbroken for almost 30m. It is possible to follow a rocky ledge behind the curtain of water, but be aware that the cliffs above are unstable.

A steep path climbs out of the gorge to a car park at the top. The hard work done, we return to the country park along a pleasant mix of lanes, field paths and bridle tracks.

CRIBARTH & HENRHYD FALLS

DISTANCE: 13.2KM/8.2MILES » **TOTAL ASCENT:** 572M/1,877FT » **START GR:** SN 839155 » **TIME:** ALLOW 4.5 HOURS **MAP:** OS EXPLORER OL12, BRECON BEACONS NATIONAL PARK WESTERN AREA, 1:25,000 » **REFRESHMENTS:** CHANGING SEASONS TEA ROOMS & RESTAURANT, CRAIG-Y-NOS COUNTRY PARK; PENYCAE INN, PEN-Y-CAE » **NAVIGATION:** GENERALLY CLEAR PATHS, THOUGH CARE SHOULD BE TAKEN ON CRIBARTH IN POOR VISIBILITY.

HENRHYD FALLS PHOTO: TRACY BURTON

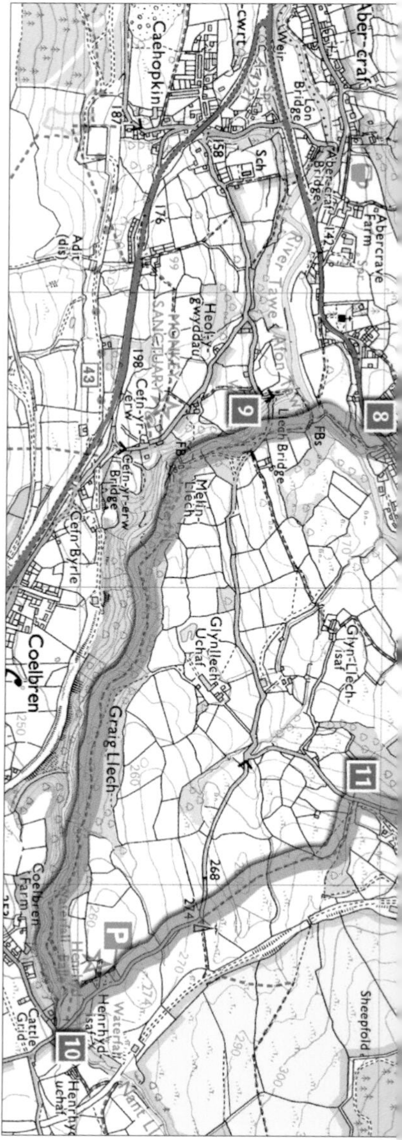

17 CRIBARTH & HENRHYD FALLS

Directions – Cribarth & Henrhyd Falls

S Leave the car park by the main entrance/exit and **turn left** along the road. **Ignore** the first footpath sign on the right and continue past Craig-y-nos Castle. At a 40mph speed limit sign, **turn right** onto a grassy track, signed *Geological Trail* and *To Open Hill.* A short distance ahead, **turn right** again, onto a narrow stepped path signed *To Open Hill.*

2 Climb through thickly vegetated slopes above Craig-y-nos Castle to an open area crossed by a fence. **Turn left** and follow the fence steeply uphill. Cross a dry-stone wall ahead by a ladder stile and **turn right**. Follow the wall up over a limestone crag and down the other side.

3 Just before a metal gate on the right, **turn sharp left** onto a grassy path and climb gently towards the craggy outcrops of Cribarth. Keep **straight ahead** across the grassy bed of a former tramroad, passing through a gap in the hills with higher ground to your right. Join a dry-stone wall and fence on the left, then **fork right**, up a grassy bank, to the trig point on the summit.

4 Keep **straight ahead** past the trig point then drop back down to the main path along the wall and fence. Follow the wall gently downhill to a corner where the grassy remains of a tramroad can be seen snaking across the hill ahead. **Ignore** the tramroad and **turn left** to a stile about 50m along the wall. Cross the stile and **bear right**. The path contours around the slope of the hill, roughly parallel to a wall and fence on the right. Shortly, **swing left** and descend to a small marker post. **Bear right** from here to a stile.

5 **Do not** cross the stile, but **turn left**, following a sign for *Ynyswen*. Descend across a heathery, boulder-strewn landscape to a junction of paths by a marker post. Keep **straight ahead** towards a section of boardwalk and a stile leading into a field.

6 Cross the stile and keep **straight ahead** along the right edge of the field. Cross a stile at the end of the field and **turn right** onto a track. Go through a gateway into woodland and immediately **fork left**.

7 Descend through woodland to a stream and cross over. **Ignore** the stile ahead and **turn right**, heading more steeply downhill between the stream and a fence. At the bottom woodland edge, keep **straight ahead** across a grassy area (there is a stone stable on the left) to a metal gate. Go through and join a tarmac path between houses.

8 **Turn left** at a road, then **immediately right**. **Curve right** to a dead end, then **turn left** down a short section of path to a main road. Follow the pavement **left** for a few metres, then cross to a metal gate signed *Henrhyd Waterfall*. Follow a path down to the River Tawe. Cross a footbridge over the river, then **fork left** up steps. Climb to a road and **turn right**. A short distance down the hill, **turn left** onto a path signed *Waterfall*.

9 Follow an undulating path up the wooded Nant Llech gorge, negotiating a number of boardwalks, footbridges, stiles and steps. After some 2km, you will emerge at a junction with a wider gravel path. Keep **straight ahead** along the lower, riverside path to view the waterfall. Return the same way, this time **turning right** at the junction and climbing steeply to a car park at the top of the falls.

10 **Turn left** onto a lane and continue as far as a mast on a left-hand bend. Keep **straight ahead** over a metal stile into a field and **bear slightly left** across rough, boggy pasture to drop to a footbridge. Continue in the same direction to reach the remains of a stile, then head gently uphill towards the right-hand end of a line of trees. **Bear right** along a fence, then **left**, in the direction of a waymark arrow on an old gatepost. The path is channelled between a fence and gully and drops to a stile and lane.

11 **Turn right** and descend towards Pen-y-cae. Where the road swings left to cross the River Tawe, **bear right** onto a smaller tarmac lane towards a house. **Ignore** the continuation of the tarmac drive through a gateway and follow a bridleway sign onto a narrow, enclosed track below trees.

12 Keep **straight ahead** onto a lane, then **straight ahead** again at a wider road. Just after passing a house on the right with a well in the garden, **fork left** downhill onto a narrower lane. At a house at the end of the lane, **fork left** through a metal gate onto an enclosed track. Continue as far as a fork near the River Tawe, where the *Beacons Way* is signed in both directions.

13 **Bear left** at the fork and drop to a ford and bridge across the river. **Do not** cross, but **turn left**, following a *Beacons Way* marker along the river as far as the next footbridge. Cross here and **turn right** for a short distance to a lake near the park entrance. **Turn left** in front of the lake, then **left again** to return to the car park.

PICWS DU PHOTO: TRACY BURTON

18 Glyntawe & the 'Fans'

18.7km/11.6miles

Into the heart of the Black Mountain and back across its highest peaks.

Tafarn-y-Garreg (Glyntawe) » Cwm Haffes » Afon Twrch » Waun Lefrith (677m) » Picws Du (749m) » Fan Foel (781m) » Fan Brycheiniog (802m) » Llyn y Fan Fawr » Tafarn-y-Garreg (Glyntawe)

Start

Car park opposite the Tafarn-y-Garreg pub. A fee is payable to the pub owner. GR: SN 848171.

The Walk

No other walk in the National Park provides quite such a sense of remote mountain wilderness as this classic Black Mountain circuit. From the upper Swansea Valley, we follow a bridleway into the heart of this vast upland massif, returning across the spectacular escarpment of Bannau Sir Gaer. Llyn y Fan Fawr and a pleasant mountain stream conclude the day.

We begin from the car park opposite the Tafarn-y-Garreg pub. A short distance down the main road, we turn into Cwm Haffes and cross the boulder-strewn Haffes river below a rocky gorge. A clear grassy bridleway climbs through an undulating landscape of shake holes and limestone outcrops to the River Giedd. Between here and a second river, the Twrch, the path becomes boggier and more vague. Crossing the latter may also present some difficulty if water levels are high.

A short distance past a third stream (Nant Lluestau), we strike north across open moorland towards the summit of Waun Lefrith, the lowest and most westerly of the Bannau Sir Gaer or Carmarthen Fans. From the escarpment edge just beyond the summit cairn there are spectacular views across Llyn y Fan Fach, the first of two upland lakes to be encountered.

Turning east, we follow the escarpment edge across the 'Fans': Picws Du, Fan Foel and, highest of all, Fan Brycheiniog. A further summit, Fan Hir, is bypassed in favour of a more varied route down to Llyn y Fan Fawr and along the banks of Nant Tawe Fechan. This tumbling stream follows a course below and parallel to the long, towering ridge of Fan Hir. A rough, narrow path takes us around the southern end of the ridge to a farm (Ty Henry) and a grassy track leading back to the car park.

GLYNTAWE & THE 'FANS'

DISTANCE: 18.7KM/11.6MILES » **TOTAL ASCENT:** 809M/2,654FT » **START GR:** SN 848171 » **TIME:** ALLOW 6.5 HOURS
MAP: OS EXPLORER OL12, BRECON BEACONS NATIONAL PARK WESTERN AREA, 1:25,000 » **REFRESHMENTS:** TAFARN-Y-GARREG AND GWYN ARMS, GLYNTAWE » **NAVIGATION:** INDISTINCT AND UNDEFINED PATHS IN PLACES; MAP AND COMPASS REQUIRED.

FAN FOEL PHOTO: TRACY BURTON

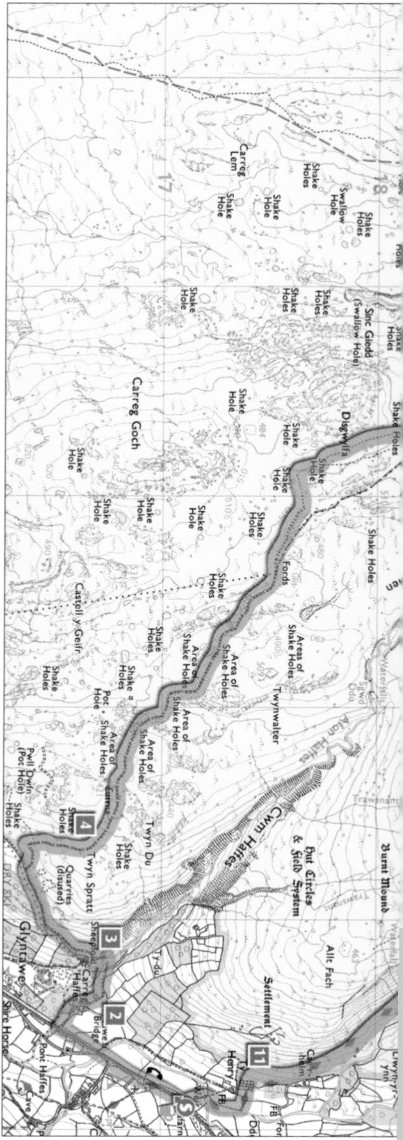

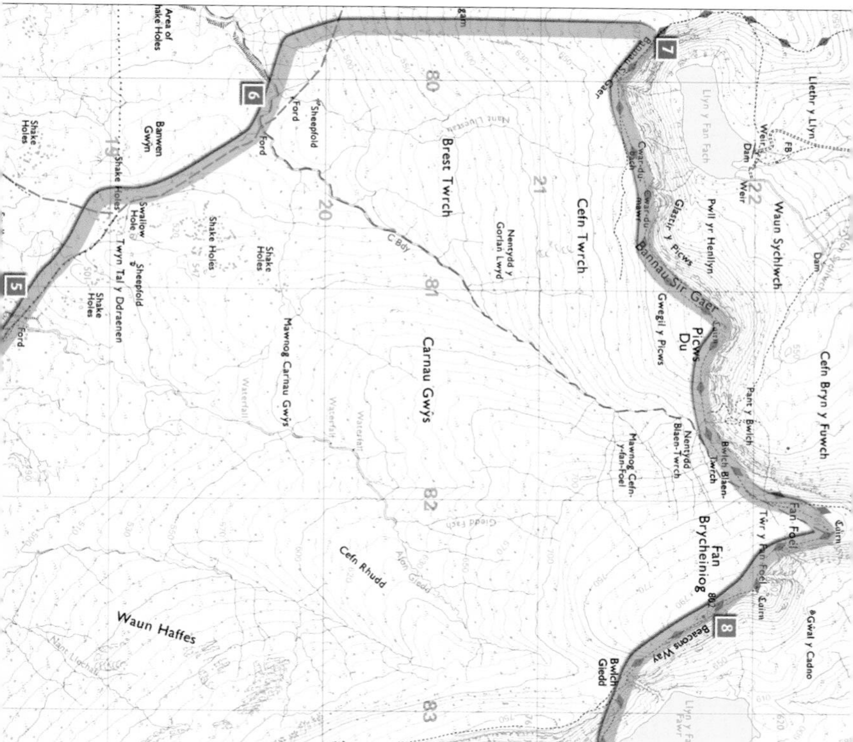

18 GLYNTAWE & THE 'FANS'

Directions – Glyntawe & the 'Fans'

S **Turn right** out of the pub car park and follow the main road down the valley. Just after the Gwyn Arms, **turn right** up an access lane to a farm, passing a sign: *Danger Crossing River in Flood.*

2 At the back of the farm, **bear left** across a gate/stile. Keep ahead, then **turn left** across a gate/stile onto a grassy path below trees. The River Haffes is met as it emerges from a narrow gorge. **Bear right** across the first small stream to an island of tussocky grassy, then use large stones in the main channel to cross to the far bank.

3 An obvious path **climbs left**, away from the river. **Swing right** by some old sheep pens and continue uphill along the base of the common. As you come to the end of a steep climb, with the bottom edge of the common curving slightly left ahead, **fork right** onto an unsigned grassy path towards rocky crags. The path curves left and then right, now heading **north** with the crags to the left.

4 At a flat, grassy area, the path curves left, now following a clear line as it trends upwards through a landscape of shake holes and limestone outcrops. Once past a large area of fenced-off bogland (Waun Fignen Felen), the path is less obvious, but intermittent white posts mark the correct route. Descend past a large pool (Pwll y Cig) and cross a small stream. A larger stream a short distance ahead is Afon Giedd.

5 Climb out of the river valley and **fork left**, in the direction of a marker post. Once over the crest of the hill, follow the clear path curving right into the Twrch valley (there are posts below to the left, but these no longer appear to be marking a used route). As you drop towards the river, the line of the path becomes uncertain.

6 If required, walk upstream until you can find a safe, dry place to cross, then follow the river downstream until a smaller watercourse (Nant Lluestau) joins from the right. Cross over and follow a path up the slope ahead. Once above the boggier lower slopes, **strike out right** towards a line of crags. At the top, head **due north** across open moorland towards the summit of Waun Lefrith.

7 From the summit, **turn right** and follow the edge of the towering escarpment above Llyn y Fan Fach. After a steady climb across Picws Du, the path drops steeply into Bwlch Blaen-Twrch. There is then a steep pull, stepped in places, to the summit of Fan Foel. **Curve right** from here, climbing gently past a cairn to a trig point marking the summit of Fan Brycheiniog.

8 Descend into Bwlch Giedd, then **drop left** down a steep path to Llyn y Fan Fawr. Just before reaching the shore, **turn right** along the base of the Fan Hir escarpment. There is no one clear path at first, but aim for a long ridge of moraine along the escarpment base. Follow a path along the crest of the ridge, then drop steeply to join the left bank of a stream.

9 The path descends to a ford above a waterfall. If water levels are high, cross here and continue down the opposite bank. Otherwise, continue along the left bank (fine views of waterfalls) to a lower crossing point above a gorge. This can be more difficult to cross when the river is in spate.

10 Once over, join a rough path across the slope towards the line of a wall/fence. Follow the edge of the common down to a high bank above the river. **Do not** go through a small metal gate ahead, but **bear right** onto a rough path alongside a wall.

11 With a large concrete sheep pen ahead, **turn left** over a stile marked *Beacons Way*. **Bear right**, then **left** through a gateway. Descend on a grassy track between fences to the River Tawe and **turn right**. Cross the river at a footbridge and shortly emerge in the Tafarn-y-Garreg car park.

BANNAU SIR GAER AND FAN FOEL FROM LLANDDEUSANT PHOTO: ADAM LONG

19 The Llanddeusant Circuit

15.6km/9.7miles

A walk on the wild side through Cwm Sawdde Fechan and across the limestone pavements of Garreg Las.

Llanddeusant » Cwm Sawdde Fechan » Blaenllynfell » Garreg Las (635m) » Carreg yr Ogof (585m) » Llanddeusant

Start

Information board outside Llanddeusant Church. There is limited roadside parking along adjacent lanes. It may be possible to park in the youth hostel car park, but please ask for permission first.
GR: SN 776245.

The Walk

Llanddeusant ('church of the two saints') is a small group of houses around a church and former pub (now a youth hostel) on the edge of the Black Mountain. Our walk heads south from the village, climbing steadily along the narrow valley of Cwm Sawdde Fechan and returning across the limestone pavements of Garreg Las. Rugged terrain and indistinct paths make this a fine weather walk only.

Quiet lanes lead to a muddy track onto the common. Once past a pleasant stream, we pick our way over rough moorland, tracing a narrow, indistinct path into Cwm Sawdde Fechan. This continues up the valley, dipping in and out of numerous side gullies, then crosses the Sawdde Fechan stream.

An area of flat moorland marks the Black Mountain watershed and we can now move more swiftly towards the limestone crags of Garreg Las on our left. Although we have joined the Beacons Way, there are no signs to indicate this, and the path remains faint and indistinct.

Garreg Las is a ridge of jagged limestone pavements that can be treacherously slippery when wet. Sticking to the higher ground on its western side, we avoid the most difficult boulder fields and climb steadily towards two cairns (Carnau'r Garreg Las) at the north end of the ridge. From here we can appreciate the full extent of this wild, remote region.

We soon pass the trig point on Carreg yr Ogof and begin a long descent into the Sawdde valley. Before long we join a grassy bridleway, which descends steeply to a lane and a final tarmac climb back to Llanddeusant.

THE LLANDDEUSANT CIRCUIT

DISTANCE: 15.6KM/9.7MILES » **TOTAL ASCENT:** 585M/1,919FT » **START GR:** SN 776245 » **TIME:** ALLOW 5 HOURS **MAP:** OS EXPLORER OL12, BRECON BEACONS NATIONAL PARK WESTERN AREA, 1:25,000 » **REFRESHMENTS:** NONE ON ROUTE; SMALL CAFE 2KM TO EAST OF VILLAGE LINKED TO BLAENAU FARM CAMPSITE » **NAVIGATION:** INDISTINCT AND UNDEFINED PATHS MAKE THIS A WALK FOR GOOD VISIBILITY ONLY.

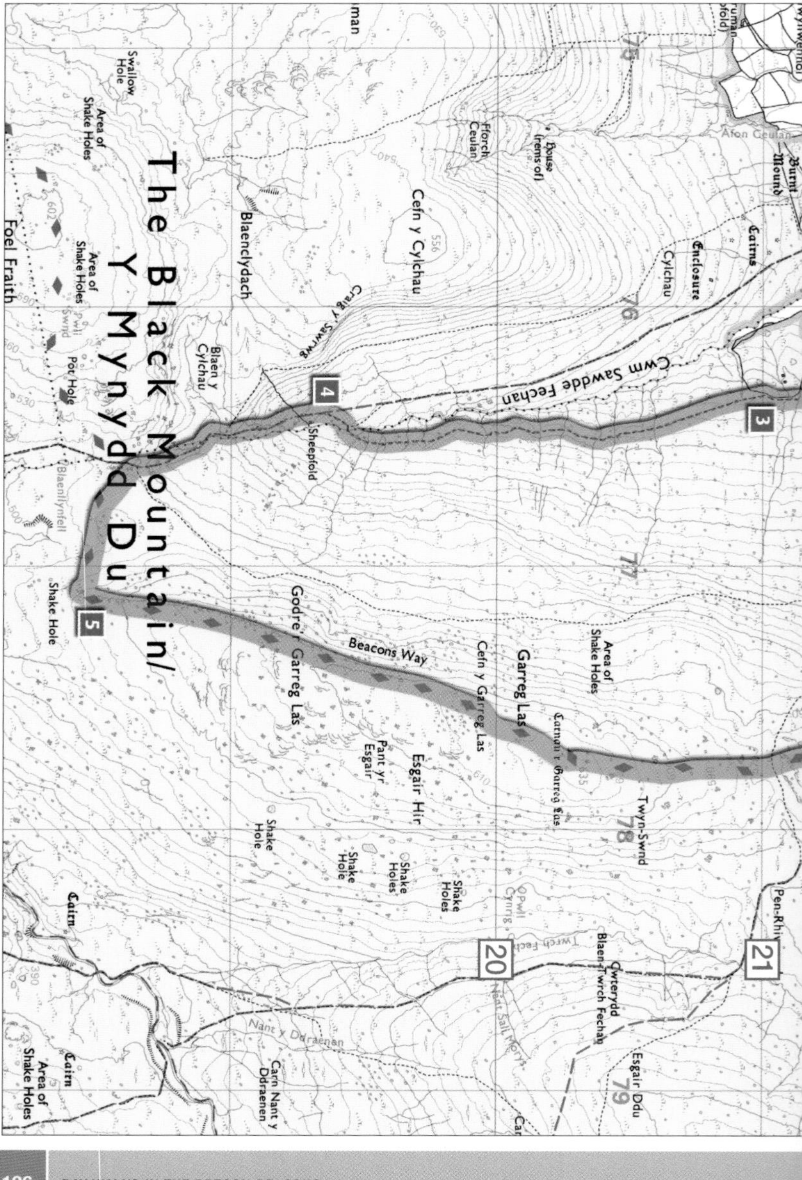

The Black Mountain/
Y Mynydd Du
Cwm Sawdde Fechan
Beacons Way
Garreg Las
Cefn y Garreg Las
Godre'r Garreg Las
Esgair Hir
Pant yr Esgair
Twyn-Swnd
Cefn y Cylchau
Blaenclydach
Blaen y Cylchau
Sheepfold
Ffrorch Ceulan
Afon Ceulan
Burnt Mound
Cairns
Enclosure
Cylchau
Swallow Hole
Area of Shake Holes
Pot Hole
Foel Fraith
Blaenllynfell
Shake Hole
Shake Holes
Cairn
Carn Nant y Ddraenen
Nant y Ddraenen
Blaen-Twrch Fechan
Esgair Ddu
Pen-Rhiw
Pwll Cynnig
Twrch Fechan
Nant Sali Morys
Carnau'r Garreg Las
3
4
5
20
21
75
76
77
78
79
556
602
610
635

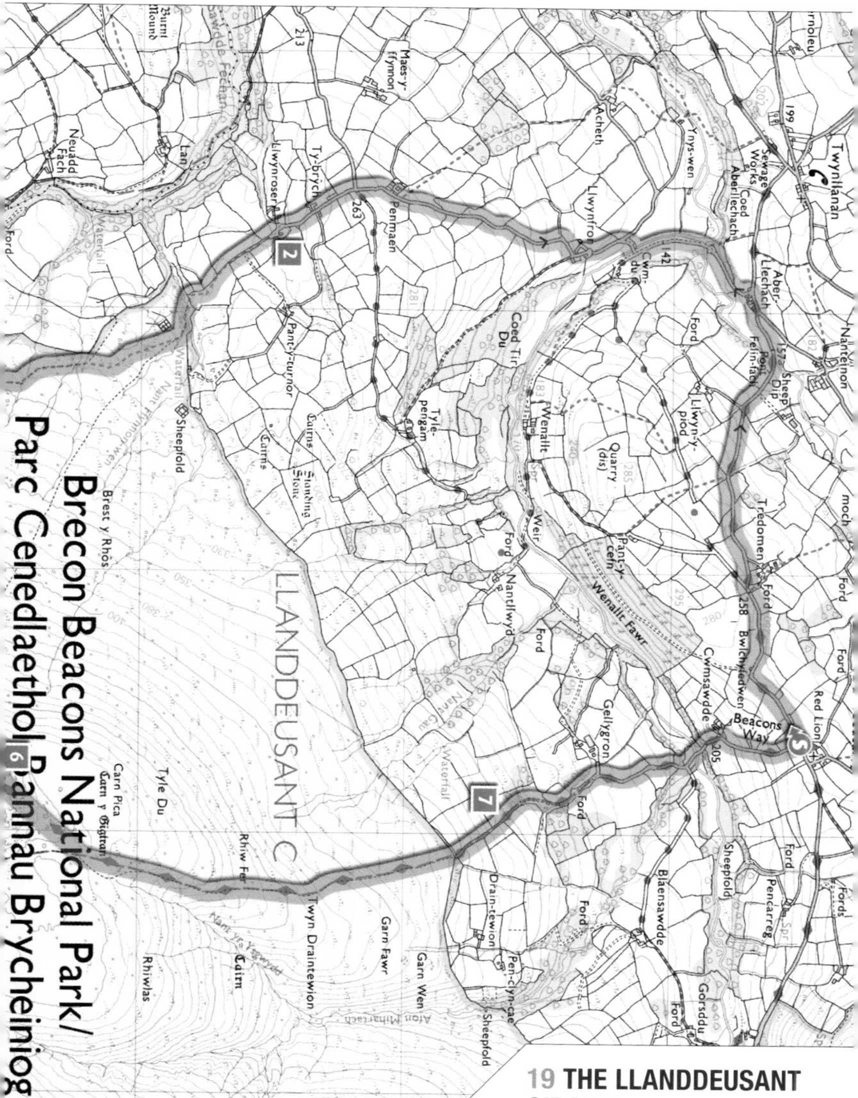

19 THE LLANDDEUSANT CIRCUIT

Directions – The Llanddeusant Circuit

S With your back to Llanddeusant Church, **turn right** along the lane heading west towards Twynllanan. After about 2km, **turn left** by a large house. The lane turns sharply right to cross a river, then curves left and begins to climb steeply. Where the main lane turns right at the top of the hill, keep **straight ahead** in the direction of the Black Mountain.

2 At the end of the lane, follow waymarks onto a muddy track to the common. Cross a pretty stream along the edge of the common and **climb left** out of the valley. Once on the open hill, **bear slightly right**, so as to keep roughly parallel with the common boundary. Keep heading south, towards the V-shaped valley of Cwm Sawdde Fechan, passing close to a fence and wall on the right.

3 The rough path continues south along the valley wall, dipping in and out of numerous little gullies on the way. Eventually, drop to the stream and cross to the opposite bank about 100m or so below the remains of an old stone enclosure (marked *Sheepfold* on OS map).

4 Follow the stream past a number of small waterfalls and climb steeply up the valley headwall. Where the gradient lessens, join a more obvious track and continue south across a large flat area of open moorland. **Bear left** where convenient towards the right-hand end of the rocky ridge to the east.

5 **Turn left** and climb across the limestone pavement of Godre'r Garreg Las. Stick to the highest ground to avoid difficult boulder fields, then aim for a cairn at the higher, northern end of the ridge. Pass a second cairn just behind the first, then drop into the saddle between Garreg Las and Carreg yr Ogof. Climb gently to the summit of the latter, which is marked by a trig point.

6 The way down from Carreg yr Ogof is not immediately clear. **Bear right** (north-east) to meet a grassy bridleway descending north off the mountain (the distant church in Llanddeusant provides a good landmark). A clear path drops to the edge of the common and continues as a sunken green lane between banks.

7 Descend steeply to a stony track and continue downhill. **Turn right** at a T-junction with a lane and descend again to a bridge over Afon Sawdde. The lane climbs steeply from the river to Llanddeusant.

LLANDDEUSANT CHURCH PHOTO: ADAM LONG

DYFFRYN TYWI FROM CARN GOCH PHOTO: TRACY BURTON

20 Carn Goch & Carreg Cennen Castle

18.3km/11.3miles

A spectacular hilltop castle and the largest Iron Age hillfort in Wales.

Carn Goch » Bwlch y Gors » Banc Wernwgan » Carreg Cennen Castle » Carn Goch

Start

Grassy lay-by at the western end of Carn Goch. GR: SN 681242.

The Walk

This moderately strenuous walk uses a mixture of lanes, tracks and field paths to connect two hilltop fortifications – Carn Goch and Carreg Cennen Castle – on the western edge of the National Park. Although we never climb above 350m, there are fine views to savour as well as considerable historical interest.

We begin below Carn Goch, a hill consisting of two linked forts, Y Gaer Fach and Y Gaer Fawr, that together comprise the largest Iron Age fortification in Wales. A clear path leads up through the ramparts, but it is the view from the top that takes the breath away: the bleak slopes of the Black Mountain rising behind and Dyffryn Tywi's patchwork pattern of lush green farmland below.

Leaving Carn Goch, we join a track climbing steadily across the shoulder of Trichrug before dropping into a maze of narrow country lanes. There follows some 4km of road walking, but on lanes so quiet we may not meet a single vehicle. Climbing towards Banc Wernwgan, we should catch our first glimpse of Carreg Cennen Castle, a striking medieval stronghold spectacularly located above a sheer limestone precipice.

Tracks and rough paths drop steeply to a bridge across Afon Cennen. From here, a well-graded path climbs through a lovely mix of deciduous woodland to the castle gates. If time allows, it is worth paying the price of admission. Outside the castle walls are toilets and tearooms at the nearby Castell Farm.

The return to Carn Goch is mainly along the Beacons Way, but to avoid retracing our steps over Carn Goch, we choose a more direct line back from Carreglwyd Wood, along the field path descending north-west to a lane.

CARN GOCH & CARREG CENNEN CASTLE

DISTANCE: 18.3KM/11.3MILES » **TOTAL ASCENT:** 568M/1,864FT » **START GR:** SN 681242 » **TIME:** ALLOW 6 HOURS **MAP:** OS EXPLORER OL12, BRECON BEACONS NATIONAL PARK WESTERN AREA, 1:25,000 » **REFRESHMENTS:** CASTELL FARM CAFE, CARREG CENNEN CASTLE » **NAVIGATION:** MOSTLY CLEAR LANES AND TRACKS, BUT SOME UNDEFINED FIELD PATHS MAY REQUIRE MAP WORK.

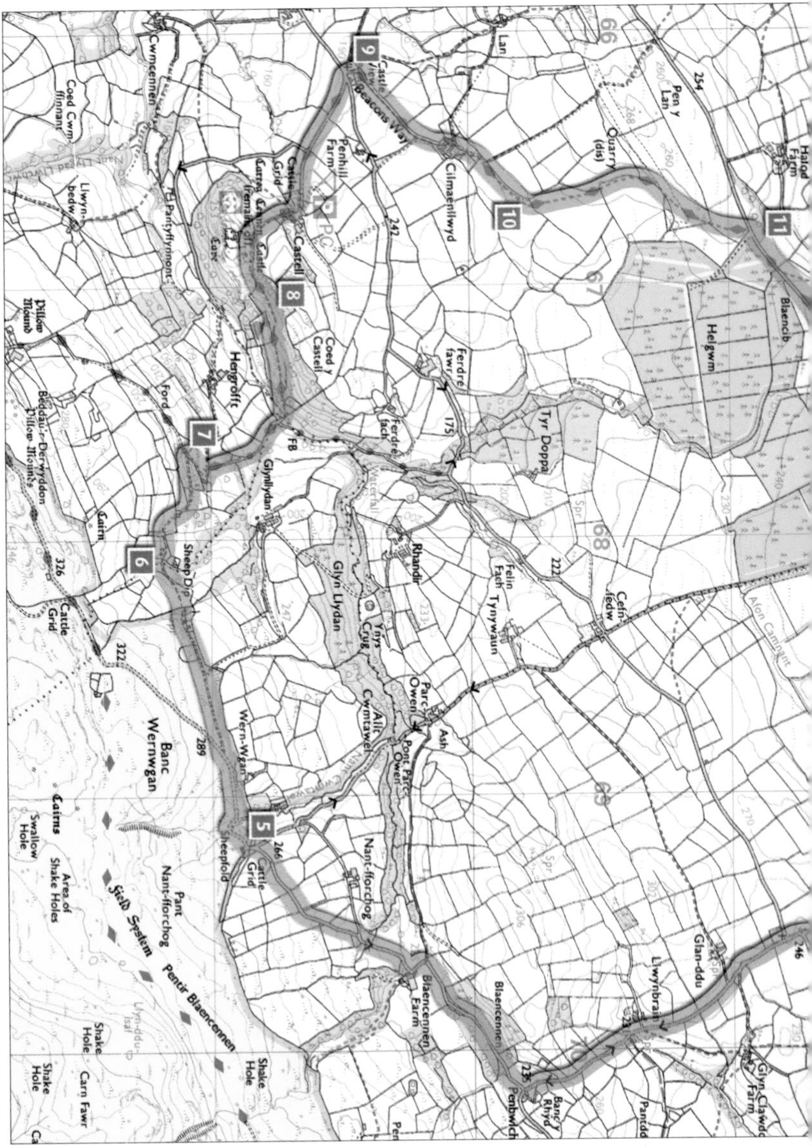
Cwmcennen
Coed Cwm-ffinnant
Llwyn-bedw
Pantyffynnont
Pillow Mound
Beddau'r-Derwyddon
Pillow Mounds
Cairn
Castle View
Beacons Way
Penhill Farm
Cattle Grid
Carreg Cennen Castle (remains of)
Cave
Castell
Coed y Castell
Hengrofft
Ford
FB
Glynllydan
Sheep Dip
Cattle Grid
Lan
Pen y Lan
Quarry (dis)
Cilmaenllwyd
Halod Farm
Blaencib
Helgwm
Ferdre fawr
Ferdre fach
Tyr Doppa
Waterfall
Rhandir
Glyn Llydan
Ynys Crug
Felin Fach
Tynywaun
Cefn-fedw
Afon Cennen
Parc Owen
Ash
Pont Parc Owen
Allt Cwmtawel
Nant Cwmtawel
Wern-Wgan
Banc Wernwgan
Cairns
Swallow Hole
Sheepfold
Cattle Grid
Nant-fforchog
Pant Nant-fforchog
Area of Shake Holes
Field System
Pentir Blaencennen
Shake Hole
Carn Fawr
Blaencennen Farm
Blaencennen
Glan-ddu
Llwynbrain
Glyn Clawdd Farm
Pantdd
Banc y Rhyd
Penbwlch
Spr
Llyn-ddu Isaf

20 CARN GOCH & CARREG CENNEN CASTLE

Directions – Carn Goch & Carreg Cennen Castle

S From the car park, follow an obvious path up the hill. Go over Y Gaer Fach, then cross the dip towards the larger hill ahead, Y Gaer Fawr. **Curve left** across boulders onto the summit plateau and head for the far (north-eastern) end of the fort.

2 From a gap in the outer ramparts, a clear track **curves right**, dropping across the hill to meet a lane opposite a farm track. **Turn right** along the lane and continue through a gate onto a gravel track. Almost immediately, **fork left** onto an enclosed path between hedges.

3 The track climbs steadily, then curves right to meet a junction of tracks. **Turn right** and follow a wide track uphill to a junction of paths and tracks west of Trichrug. **Ignore** the *Beacons Way* arrow pointing right and continue ahead along the main track. Keep **straight ahead** onto a gravel forestry road and descend to a tarmac lane.

4 At a T-junction, keep **straight ahead** onto a wider lane. Where this curves sharply right by a chapel, **bear left** (effectively straight ahead) onto a smaller lane signed to *Brynaman*. The road dips, climbs, then descends again to a T-junction. **Turn right** (signed *Ammanford*) and follow the lane up to a cattle grid on the edge of the common.

5 Go over the cattle grid and follow the unfenced road across the common. Where the road starts to bear left, up the hill, **fork right** onto a gravel vehicle track running parallel to the common boundary. Keep ahead past a house at the end of the track and drop down a grassy slope to a partially concealed gate and stile. Cross a rough field ahead to a muddy track below trees.

6 Negotiate a muddy stream and cross a stile into a field. Follow the wire fence on the right to the next stile, then **bear right** to a gate in front of a small Dutch barn. A gravel track leads gently downhill from here in the direction of Carreg Cennen Castle, now clearly visible on the hill ahead.

7 Rejoin the Beacons Way at a junction of tracks. Follow the main track downhill as it swings sharply right and then left. On the second bend, **bear right** to a stile with a red castle waymark and follow a path downhill to a bridge at the bottom. Shortly, cross a second bridge near a sign for *Carreg Cennen Wood*. **Turn right**, then **immediately left**, and climb diagonally uphill towards Carreg Cennen Castle.

8 Go through a wooden gate at the top of the climb and pass the entrance to the castle (you will need to pay to go in). Follow a tarmac path down to tearooms and farm buildings and **bear left** along the top edge of a car park (toilets and picnic tables). Leave the car park onto a narrow access road and continue to a T-junction.

9 **Turn left** onto the lane, then **immediately right** onto a gravel track. Where the main track swings left, keep **straight ahead** onto a narrower track and reach an abandoned farm. Follow the track round the farm and continue on a grassy track along the left edge of a field.

10 The track curves left to a gate. Leave the track and **head straight** up a field to a stile. Continue along the left edge of a field, then cross a stile to a grassy track on the far side of a dry-stone wall. **Turn right** along the wall to a waymark post and **follow the arrows left** across rough pasture and ferns to a gate in a stone wall. Cross by a ladder stile and walk through more rough, boggy pasture to a lane.

11 **Turn right** onto a long, straight lane, climbing steadily for over 1km. At a junction of lanes, cross over and continue along a wide, grassy track ahead. This joins the right side of a fence as far as a forestry plantation. Follow the obvious path gently downhill through the trees to meet a forestry track in a clearing. **Bear left** across the track and continue to descend.

12 With a gate ahead, **ignore** a Beacons Way arrow pointing uphill to the right. Instead, go through the gate and **turn immediately left**, down the edge of the wood. At the bottom, **continue ahead** through rough fields until a waymark arrow directs you to **bear left**, towards the far corner of a field. Follow the next field down to a cottage and **bear left** to a gate onto a lane. **Turn right** along the lane, following it sharp left then sharp right, to return to your starting point.

Also by
Vertebrate Publishing
Day Walks on the
SouthDowns
20 circular routes in
Hampshire & Sussex
Day Walks in the
North York Moors
20 circular routes in
North Yorkshire
Day Walks in
Snowdonia
20 circular routes in
North Wales
Day Walks in the
PeakDistrict
20 classic circular routes
Order direct from www.v-publishing.co.uk

Appendix

The following is a list of Tourist Information Centres, shops, cafes, pubs, websites and other contacts that might come in handy.

Tourist Information Centres

www.breconbeacons.org

Abergavenny	T: 01873 853 254
Blaenavon	T: 01495 742 333
Brecon	T: 01874 622 485
Brynaman	T: 01269 823 400
Craig-y-nos	T: 01639 730 395
Crickhowell	T: 01873 811 970
Hay-on-Wye	T: 01497 820 144
Libanus	T: 01874 623 366
Llandovery	T: 01550 720 693
Merthyr Tydfil	T: 01685 727 474
Pontneddfechan	T: 01639 721 795
Talgarth	T: 01874 712 226

Food and Drink

Cafes

(See individual routes for recommendations.)

The Lakeside Restaurant
Llangors T: 01874 658 170

The Old Barn Tearooms
Ystradgynwyn T: 01685 383 358

National Park Visitor Centre & Tea Rooms,
Libanus T: 01874 623 366

Changing Seasons Tea Rooms & Restuarant,
Craig-y-nos Country Park T: 01639 731 498

Castell Farm Cafe
Carreg Cennen Castle T: 01558 822 291

Pubs

(See individual routes for recommendations.)

Skirrid Mountain Inn
Llanvihangel Crucorney T: 01873 890 258

The Red Lion – Llanbedr T: 01873 810 754

Llanthony Priory Hotel
Llanthony T: 01873 890 487

The Dragons Back
Pengenffordd T: 01874 711 353

The Castle Inn – Llangors T: 01874 658 819

The Red Lion – Llangynidr T: 01874 730 223

The Coach & Horses
Llangynidr T: 01874 730 245

The White Swan
Llanfrynach T: 01874 665 277

Old White Horse Inn
Pontneddfechan T: 01639 721 173

The Angel Inn
Pontneddfechan T: 01639 722 013

Tafarn-y-Garreg
Glyntawe T: 01639 731 415

Gwyn Arms – Glyntawe T: 01639 730 310

Accommodation

Youth Hostels

YHA Youth Hostels can be found in the following places. For more information please visit: **www.yha.org.uk**

Danywenallt	T: 0845 371 9548
Llanddeusant	T: 0845 371 9750
Llangattock Mountain Bunkhouse	T: 01873 812 307
Brecon Beacons	T: 0845 371 9029

Bunkhouses, B&Bs and Hotels

www.breconbeaconstourism.co.uk

For further information, contact a Tourist Information Centre in the area in which you intend to stay.

Camping

www.camping-wales.co.uk

Provides a good overview of the campsites available in the Brecon Beacons National Park. For more information, contact a local Tourist Information Centre.

Weather

www.metoffice.gov.uk

Provides a mountain area forecast for the Brecon Beacons.

Outdoor Shops

Crickhowell Adventure – High Street, Crickhowell
T: **01873 810 020**
Cotswold Outdoor – The Struet, Brecon
T: **01874 622 551** **www.cotswoldoutdoor.com**
Gibb Outdoors – High Street, Brecon
T: **01874 622 949** **www.gibboutdoors.co.uk**
The Camp Shop – Sennybridge
T: **01874 638 145**

Other Publications

Day Walks in Snowdonia
Tom Hutton, Vertebrate Publishing – **www.v-publishing.co.uk**

Wales Mountain Biking / Beicio Mynydd Cymru
Tom Hutton, Vertebrate Publishing – **www.v-publishing.co.uk**

Mountain Biking Trail Centres – The Guide
Tom Fenton, Vertebrate Publishing – **www.v-publishing.co.uk**

Great Britain Mountain Biking
Tom Fenton & Andy McCandlish, Vertebrate Publishing – **www.v-publishing.co.uk**

Great British Bike Rides
Dave Barter, Vertebrate Publishing – **www.v-publishing.co.uk**

About the Author

Harri Roberts is a freelance writer, editor and translator based in Newport, Gwent. He has authored a number of Welsh walking guides, including an official guide to the Wales Coast Path (Tenby to Swansea section), and runs an e-publishing company called *camau* (Welsh for 'steps') with his partner Tracy. His love of the Brecon Beacons developed during research for an ambitious guide to the Cambrian Way, a high-level, Welsh 'end-to-end' across some of the most scenic and mountainous terrain in the country.

Vertebrate Publishing

At Vertebrate Publishing we publish books to inspire adventure.

It's our rule that the only books we publish are those that we'd want to read or use ourselves. We endeavour to bring you beautiful books that stand the test of time and that you'll be proud to have on your bookshelf for years to come.

The Peak District was the inspiration behind our first books. Our offices are situated on its doorstep, minutes away from world-class climbing, biking and hillwalking. We're driven by our own passion for the outdoors, for exploration, and for the natural world; it's this passion that we want to share with our readers.

We aim to inspire everyone to get out there. We want to connect readers – young and old – with the outdoors and the positive impact it can have on well-being. We think it's particularly important that young people get outside and explore the natural world, something we support through our publishing programme.

As well as publishing award-winning new books, we're working to make available many out-of-print classics in both print and digital formats. These are stories that we believe are unique and significant; we want to make sure that they continue to be shared and enjoyed.

www.v-publishing.co.uk